Table of Contents

I0571239

Introduction

Growing up as a gay kid in western Pennsylvania during the 1970s and 80s wasn't just hard, it was lonely and confusing. Western Pennsylvania is a unique mix of Midwestern practicality, Appalachian conservatism, and East Coast grit, and none of those perspectives made room for someone like me. I learned early on that being gay wasn't "normal" and was something to be hidden, something to feel ashamed of. And like so many others, I became an expert at pretending to be someone I wasn't.

It wasn't until I moved to Washington, DC, in the late 1980s that I finally felt free to be myself. There, I could leave behind the fear of disappointing my family or facing judgment from lifelong friends. Starting fresh gave me the chance to meet new people as my authentic self, a gay man, without apology or hesitation. For the first time, I didn't feel like I was hiding. Instead, I found acceptance, community, and a sense of belonging that I didn't even know I was missing.

Back then, there wasn't an internet to turn to for advice or representation. No YouTube, no TV shows, no magazines with gay characters who had happy endings. But in DC, I discovered The Washington Blade, a free newspaper that portrayed LGBTQ life in a positive light. It felt like a lifeline, finally, there was information on everything from HIV prevention to legal rights to local gay bars and clubs. These weren't just places to dance or drink; they were places where I met people who helped me understand myself and my place in the world. I learned that there isn't just one way to be gay. I met men who were effeminate, masculine, and everything in between. I discovered bears, twinks, preppies, and drag queens, and in every one of them, I saw the beauty of diversity.

Of course, the 1980s were also defined by the AIDS crisis. While so much of the country was consumed by ignorance and fear, the LGBTQ community in DC was at the forefront of education and prevention. I honestly believe that moving to DC saved my life. If I had stayed in Pennsylvania, I might never have learned about HIV prevention until it was too late.

Even now, with all the progress we've made, being gay can still be a challenge. Homophobia and discrimination haven't disappeared, and for many, self-acceptance is still a journey. Coming out remains one of the hardest, and most important, steps a gay man can take.

I wrote this book because I wish I'd had something like it growing up in western Pennsylvania. I want you to know that being gay is not only okay, but also a gift. It's a part of who you are, but it doesn't define you entirely. My hope is that this book will help you embrace all of who you are and remind you that you're never alone.

Chapter 1:

Accepting and Loving Yourself—The Importance of Self-Acceptance

Learning to truly accept and love yourself is one of the most crucial steps on the journey to happiness and fulfillment. As a gay man, self-acceptance means embracing your sexual orientation as a natural, healthy, and integral part of who you are. It's about recognizing that being gay is not a flaw, a phase, a choice, or anything shameful—it is simply one beautiful aspect of the multi-faceted human being that you are.

When we don't fully accept ourselves, we operate from a place of inner conflict and turmoil. We expend immense energy trying to hide, change, or resist this essential part of our identity. Thus, we are prevented from showing up authentically, cultivating genuine relationships, and going after what makes us come alive. As the pioneering gay psychotherapist Alan Downs wrote in *The Velvet Rage* (2005), "Authenticity is the only gateway to real intimacy and joy (Goodreads, n.d.)."

The key to unlocking the door to a life of freedom, wholeness, and unshakeable self-worth as a gay man is self-acceptance. With homophobia and heteronormativity so rampant in the world today, it is still a journey of courage for many of us to be loving and self-accepting of ourselves. It requires unlearning the toxic messages and fears that we have internalized and re-discovering the innate lovability that we were born with.

The good news is that, no matter what your current relationship with yourself is like, radical self-acceptance is possible. It begins with understanding that your worthiness is unconditional—it has nothing to do with whom you love. From there, it's about consciously choosing love, compassion, and respect for yourself every single time. This is not a one-time decision, but a lifelong practice.

Some key habits to cultivate on the self-acceptance path are:

Affirm Yourself Daily

Look in the mirror each morning and say, "I love and accept myself completely as a gay man." Recite Stuart Smalley's famous mantra from SNL: "I'm good enough, I'm smart enough, and doggone it, people like me!" Create your own empowering affirmations (*I Am Amazing*, 2016).

Forgive Yourself

We've all absorbed homophobic programming and acted from that wounded place. Have compassion for yourself and let go of shame and self-blame for not being further along. Trust that you're doing the best you can.

Celebrate Your Gayness

Acknowledge all the gifts, strengths, and unique perspectives you have to offer because of your sexual orientation. How has being gay made you more empathetic, resilient, and creative? Regularly appreciate these qualities.

Choose Gay-affirming Media, Role Models and Environments

Limit your exposure to heteronormative, homophobic content and spaces. Surround yourself with books, movies, podcasts, people, and communities that mirror your experience and uplift your gay identity.

Express Yourself Authentically

Practice letting your true gay self shine in more and more areas of life. You don't have to broadcast it everywhere, but hiding, censoring, and compartmentalizing yourself breeds shame. Live out and be proud in ways that feel good to you.

Get Support

You don't have to figure this out alone. Lean on supportive friends, family, mentors, or a therapist. Join a gay men's group. Consider a personal growth workshop like The Breakthrough in LA or GALA in the UK, designed for gay men.

Remember, self-acceptance isn't a feeling that arrives one day and remains forever. Self-acceptance is an intentional way of treating yourself—a practice you commit to every single day. The more you flex this muscle, the easier and more natural it becomes. You strengthen the grooves of self-love each time you choose it.

And the beautiful ripple effect is that the more you accept yourself, the more you give others permission to do the same. When you embody self-acceptance, you become a role model and light the way for other gay men to unapologetically step into their truth. As Harvey Milk said, "Hope will never be silent."

Overcoming Internalized Homophobia and Shame

For many gay men, the biggest barrier to self-acceptance and happiness isn't the homophobia we encounter out in the world—it's the homophobia we've internalized and carry inside ourselves. Internalized homophobia refers to the negative beliefs, stereotypes, and stigma about homosexuality that we've absorbed from society and adopted as our own.

It's the voice inside that says there's something wrong with or shameful about being gay. That we're not "man enough," that we're dirty, sinful, or sick. We're doomed to a life of loneliness, rejection, or marginalization. Even if we intellectually know better, these harmful messages can persist in our psyche on a visceral level.

Internalized homophobia is a direct consequence of growing up in a culture that privileges heterosexuality and treats any deviation as abnormal, inferior, or downright shameful. From a young age, we learn that being gay is bad. Parents, teachers, religious leaders, politicians, and even the media will pass on the same message. Additionally, even if others have stopped speaking against it as time has passed, the silence around gayness speaks volumes.

So, as gay boys and men, we learn to reject and repress this core part of ourselves. We develop sophisticated strategies of hiding, overcompensating, or lashing out at other gays to protect ourselves from this stigma. We may throw ourselves into school, work, or other "masculine" pursuits to prove our worth and distract from our gayness. We may try to "pass" as straight, pursue conversion therapy, or enter into heterosexual relationships to quell the gay inside.

By attempting to protect ourselves from external hurt and rejection, we end up rejecting and betraying ourselves. We fragment and go to war with our very beings, which breeds a profound sense of shame, unworthiness, and a feeling of deep fraud. This constant inner conflict diminishes our ability to lead joyful, fulfilling lives and connect with others on a deep level.

In order for us to be happy, we must first heal these internalized wounds. We have to uproot the lies we've come to believe about our innate lovability (or lack thereof). We have to reclaim the beautiful, worthy essence beneath the shame and self-attack.

Some steps to help with this lifelong process are:

Develop Awareness

Notice your negative self-talk and beliefs about being gay. Write them down. Question whether they're actually true. Look for evidence of the opposite—your goodness, desirability, and okayness.

Feel Your Feelings

Allow yourself to feel the anger, grief, and fear underneath your shame. Cry, scream into a pillow, and move your body. Locate the feeling and breathe through it. This helps digest the pain so it doesn't drive your behavior unconsciously.

Re-parent Yourself

Be the loving, accepting parent to yourself that you may not have had. Tell your younger self the messages of affirmation he needs to hear. "You are lovable and worthy, just as you are. There's nothing wrong with being gay."

Get Educated

Read books, watch movies, and attend talks that uplift and normalize the gay experience. Immerse yourself in gay history and culture. The more knowledge you gain, the greater your ability to recognize the lies that were previously fed to you. This is why knowledge is power!

Cultivate Gay Community

Spend time with other gay men who are proud of who they are. Receive their mirroring, support, and validation. If you don't have access to the community in person, find it online. Simply knowing that you're not alone can be a powerful medicine.

Work With a Therapist

Internalized homophobia can be deeply rooted and challenging to unpack on your own. A skilled LGBT therapist can help you identify your negative beliefs and reframe them. Such a therapist will help you to experience being seen and accepted by both yourself and by society at large.

Practice Self-Compassion

Internalized homophobia is not your fault—it's the product of growing up in a heteronormative world. Be kind, patient, and forgiving of yourself—and of any mistakes you may have made along the way—as you heal and transform such a feeling. You're doing sacred work.

Affirm Your Gayness

Affirm your gayness and develop a positive gay identity based on self-love and celebration. Try to collect images and quotes and look up role models that may uplift your spirits and teach you to stand proud of your gayness. Take in the affirmation that you're a gift to the world exactly as you are.

Overcoming internalized homophobia is a courageous, ongoing journey. It takes tremendous inner work to unlearn the toxic conditioning of a lifetime and recover our innate wholeness. But with commitment, support, and lots of self-compassion, it's absolutely possible.

As we slowly learn to heal our shame and cultivate genuine self-love, we also experience the greatest amount of freedom and peace. We also tend to show up more fully in our relationships and pursuits. We tap into our unique creativity and self-expression and are able to build the authentic, vibrant lives we deserve as gay men.

Audre Lorde wrote, "Shame is the lie someone told you about yourself (Goodreads, n.d.)." This has never been more true in a heteronormative culture that has shamed gayness for centuries. But you don't have to carry this lie a moment longer. Commit now to telling yourself a radically different story—that you are lovable, worthy, and more than enough, exactly as you are. As more gay men start believing this truth, we will help to create a world of compassion for all.

Developing a Positive Gay Identity

A key aspect of self-acceptance and happiness as a gay man is cultivating a positive identity around your sexual orientation. This means moving beyond just tolerating or "accepting" your homosexuality and truly embracing and celebrating it as a valued part of who you are.

Developing a positive gay identity means recognizing that being gay is not a limitation or liability but rather a unique strength and perspective you bring to the world. You must work to turn those feelings of shame and inferiority into those of pride and worthiness. It's coming to see your gayness not as something to hide or overcome but as a beautiful thread in the tapestry of your humanity.

For many of us, this is a profound paradigm shift from the negative self-image(s) that we have somehow internalized. We've been taught that gayness is a defect, a perversion, and a one-way ticket to misery and isolation. Even if we don't buy into the most blatant stereotypes, we may still carry an underlying sense that we're 'less than' because of our sexual orientation.

Challenging these beliefs and assumptions is at the heart of developing a gay-positive identity. It requires us to be willing and open to questioning everything we've been taught about gender, sexuality, and relationships. We need to start recognizing the ways we've been limited by heteronormative standards and ideals. To get curious about what being gay really means to us beyond the cultural baggage and projections.

Things You Need to Remember

Some important aspects of developing a positive gay identity are:

- Educate yourself about gay history and culture. Learn about the trailblazers, movements, and milestones that have paved the way for LGBTQ equality. Immerse yourself in gay literature, art, music, and media. The more you understand the richness of your heritage, the more you appreciate being part of it.

- Seek out gay role models and mentors. Connect with proud gay men who embody self-love and are thriving in various domains of life. Let their example inspire you on your own path. If you don't have access to role models in person, find them in books, movies, podcasts, etc.
- Get involved in the gay community. Attend LGBTQ events, rallies, clubs, meetings, workshops, etc. Volunteer for gay-affirming organizations. Participate in gay sports leagues, choirs, theater troupes, etc. Immerse yourself in spaces where gayness is the norm and something to be celebrated.
- Develop gay friendships and support systems. Cultivate relationships with other gay men who you can be fully yourself around. Find your chosen family and lean on them for understanding, validation, and belonging. Experience the healing power of being seen and loved for all of who you are.
- Explore your unique gay identity and expression. Move beyond rigid stereotypes and discover what being gay means to you. What are your specific gifts, values, passions, and contributions as a gay man? Honor and develop them. Let yourself shine in the way only you can.
- Own your gayness unapologetically. Practice coming out and standing up for yourself in more and more areas of life. Don't hide or downplay your sexual orientation out of fear. The

more you claim it with pride, the more you give others permission to embrace their truth.

- Redefine success and happiness on your own terms. Question heteronormative scripts for how life is "supposed" to unfold (marriage, kids, picket fences). Get in touch with what lights you up and brings you alive. Create a vision for your best gay life, then start boldly living it.
- Embrace your role in the LGBTQ community. Recognize that you belong to a beautiful, diverse family with a rich legacy of resilience. Consider how you want to contribute and carry the torch forward. How can you be a source of light and inspiration for other gay men? Let this larger purpose fuel you.
- Celebrate gayness in all its many expressions. Challenge your own biases and judgments about the 'right' way to be gay (no fems, no fats, no Asians, etc.). Question the mainstream gay ideal of the young, white, abbed Adonis. Learn to see the beauty and worth in all representations of queerness.
- Ultimately, developing a positive gay identity is about coming home to yourself. It's about releasing the shame, fear, and limitation that kept you divorced from your truth and stepping into radical self-honoring and belonging. It's about realizing that you're not a broken version of a straight person; you're a whole and perfect expression of gay personhood. And that is a profound gift.

This journey of identity development is lifelong and not always linear. You may oscillate between pride and shame, clarity and confusion, but be patient and compassionate with yourself. Surround yourself with loving mirrors and keep leaning into greater and greater gay positivity. Little by little, it becomes the lens through which you meet yourself and move through the world.

And as you deepen in self-love and gay-affirming identity, an amazing thing happens: you become an agent of change and empowerment for others on the path. By embodying pride and celebrating your gayness, you give those around you permission to shine brighter too. You never know who you might inspire by being boldly, unapologetically you.

Practicing Self-Love and Self-Care

Learning to truly love and care for yourself is some of the most important work you'll ever do as a gay man. In a world that has often told us we're unlovable, disordered, and less than, reclaiming our intrinsic worthiness is a revolutionary act. It's the foundation upon which we build lives of joy, meaning, and intimate connection.

Self-love means treating ourselves with the same compassion, respect, and affection we would a dear friend or cherished partner. It's wrapping ourselves in unconditional positive regard, even and especially when we feel we've failed, fallen short, or messed up. It's the deep knowing that we're innately deserving of good things—kindness, belonging, pleasure, success, peace—just by virtue of being.

Contrary to popular misconceptions, self-love and self-care aren't just about feeling good. They're not all bubble baths and bonbons (though those have their place!). Real self-love is making choices that align with our values and serve our highest well-being. It's giving ourselves the care and nourishment we need to thrive on every level—physically, mentally, emotionally, spiritually, and relationally.

As gay men, self-love is a particular necessity, given the stigma and adversity we face just for being who we are. We've often had to be our own best friends, cheerleaders, and advocates in the absence of support or affirmation from family, faith communities, or the wider world. We've had to fight to love ourselves in a society hell-bent on convincing us we're unworthy.

What's more, the mainstream gay male culture doesn't always foster the healthiest relationship with oneself. With its emphasis on youth, beauty, sex, partying, and consumerism, it can breed insecurity, superficiality, and self-destructive tendencies if we're not mindful. Radical self-love is an antidote to the epidemic of disordered eating, substance abuse, depression, and suicide that persists in our community.

So how do we actually cultivate self-love and self-care as gay men in a world that's often hostile to both? It's an ongoing, multi-faceted practice that requires intentionality and commitment. Some key ingredients:

- Develop a self-care routine to foster self-development through adequate sleep, nutritious food, exercise, time in nature, creative self-expression, social support, and spiritual nourishment. Build your life around self-care.
- Practice self-forgiveness. Forgive yourself for the hateful messages you've internalized. Forgive yourself for the ways you've abandoned or betrayed yourself in search of belonging. Forgive yourself for not being further along in your growth

and healing. Forgiveness is a balm that allows us to begin again.

- Have your own back, stand up for yourself, and safeguard your well-being, even when it's uncomfortable to set clear boundaries. Say no to mistreatment and anything that betrays your dignity, and mix up with the people who acknowledge, and respect you as you are, and they will help you bring out the best in you.
- Affirm yourself relentlessly. Develop a repertoire of affirmations and use them liberally, especially when your inner critic rears its ugly head. "I am enough, just as I am. I am loved and lovable. I am strong and capable. I trust my path." Record yourself reciting them and play it while driving or falling asleep.
- Connect to your body. It is natural for many of us to disown our bodies and our sexual orientation in a struggle to protect ourselves. You can counter this by consciously inhabiting and honoring your physical form. Get a massage. Dance. Practice yoga. Take a sensual bath. Make love. Let your body be a source of pleasure and wisdom.
- You might find yourself all alone in a sea full of heterosexuals, but that doesn't mean that you have to muscle through difficulty alone. There are plenty of ways to heal, grow, and thrive by seeking out support and working with a therapist, coach, or mentor. You can even keep your sanity intact by attending personal growth workshops, joining a men's group, or connecting with your community.

- Honor your full humanity. You are so much more than the sexy, shiny, successful persona the gay world tends to glorify. You get to have a full range of feelings, needs, experiences, and identities. Give yourself permission to be vulnerable, messy, and multi-dimensional. Celebrate your gorgeous imperfections.
- Practice pleasure and play. As a community that has faced so much trauma and oppression, it's crucial we connect to joy, desire, and delight too. Make time for people and activities that bring you alive. Cultivate silly, sensual, and spontaneous self-expression. Let yourself receive goodness.
- Be of service. Know that you might have gone through a hell of a lot of pain and despair to arrive where you are now, i.e., a confident and proud person of the community, but besides that, you carry a responsibility to help newbies as an inspiration, a volunteer, or a mentor. Align your life with meaning and purpose by giving back to the LGBQT community.
- At its core, self-love is a homecoming. A reclaiming of the wholeness and worthiness we were born with. By treating ourselves with tenderness and respect again and again, we gradually rewire our brains and reorient our beings. We create an unshakable foundation of okayness from which to weather any storm.
- Like building any muscle, self-love develops through daily reps and consistency. It's a practice, not a destination, involving layers and steps to pass through. The invitation is to keep showing up for ourselves with as much presence and

compassion as we can muster. To trust that every act of care is planting seeds of resilience that will blossom in time.

And here's the beautiful thing: As we deepen our own self-love and care as gay men, we lift up our entire community. We model for each other what's possible. We pass on the tools and treasures gleaned from our journeys. We create a culture of radical self-acceptance in which all queer people can heal and flourish. This is the legacy we have the power to create, starting with our very next breath. What a gift to be a part of such a movement and walk through this path! Together, we reclaim the birthright of gay dignity, joy, and belonging, one loving act at a time.

Chapter 2:

Coming Out and Living Authentically

The Coming Out Process and Different Approaches

Coming out is one of the most significant milestones in a gay man's life. You have to understand that coming out or declaring your identity as gay is not one single act but a process involving mini steps for the ultimate experience of living life with an authentic identity.

The specifics of each person's coming-out process are unique and influenced by factors like age, culture, religion, family dynamics, and social environment. Some people know they're gay from a very young age; others take years or decades to recognize and embrace their sexuality, while others come out in stages—first to themselves, then close friends or siblings, then parents and extended family, and eventually more publicly. There are also some gays who remain selectively "out" in certain spheres of life.

Regardless of the path, coming out typically involves several key stages:

Self-Discovery and Acceptance

This is the process of acknowledging to yourself that you're gay or bisexual. It often starts with a vague sense of being 'different' that gradually crystallizes into recognition of same-sex attractions. For many, self-acceptance is the hardest part of coming out. It means confronting internalized homophobia and overcoming the notion that being gay is wrong, shameful, or inferior. It takes unlearning a lifetime of heteronormative conditioning to arrive at "I am gay, and that's okay."

Disclosure to Others

This stage involves sharing your sexual orientation with others in your life. Often, it starts with people you trust the most—a close friend, sibling, parent, therapist, etc.—and widens to include extended family, friends, co-workers, and the community. Disclosure usually becomes easier with practice, but it can still be daunting each time. It requires a certain willingness to be vulnerable and risk rejection for the sake of living your truth.

Living Openly

As you disclose to more and more people, you begin integrating your public and private selves. While embracing your sexuality as a fact of life, you start openly dating, socializing with other LGBTQ people, and folding your identity into conversations, activities, and relationships. You may still not be out in every single context, but overall, you're living "out and proud" as a gay man.

Within this general model, the coming-out process can take infinite forms based on each individual's circumstances and choices. Let's look at a few different approaches:

Rip-the-Bandaid-Off Approach

Some people reach a point, often after years of secrecy and shame, where they're ready to come out to everyone all at once. They're done hiding and editing themselves and want to live fully out loud; consequences be damned. You have to be mindful that this might look like a social media announcement, a mass email, or a series of rapid-fire conversations with family and friends. But it has the upside that you will be able to get it over quickly with no regard to keeping track of who knows what. The downsides are not giving people much space to react and process, and sometimes getting more backlash than anticipated.

Slow-Drip Approach

More commonly, people come out gradually over months or years. They start by telling their most trusted confidantes, then slowly widen the circle. They test the waters and build a support base before taking on riskier disclosures. Many wait until they're out of their parent's home and financially independent before coming out to the family. Others may remain selectively closed in spheres where they feel coming out would threaten their safety, livelihood, or important relationships. This approach allows more control over the process but can be taxing to sustain walls between different parts of life.

Bring-Home-a-Boyfriend Approach

Some folks' coming out is catalyzed by falling in love. When they meet someone they want to fully incorporate into their life, the costs of secrecy start to outweigh the benefits. They come out to key people in order to be able to openly date and relate to their partner. This can be a powerful impetus and support for the coming-out process. At the same time, it can be a lot of pressure on a young relationship and sometimes confusing for people to process both the coming out and the significant other.

Social-Media Approach

For digital natives, social media can especially be a primary platform for coming out. You find it more convenient to post a Facebook status, Instagram photo, or YouTube video to announce your sexual orientation to a broad audience all at once. You can keep it slow-paced with careful, tiny steps. For example, begin by changing your profile photo to a rainbow flag or sharing coming-out articles to test the waters before a bigger reveal. Social media disclosures can be a powerful way to connect with the community and assert your identity. However, they can also invite unwanted comments or speculation, which may warrant more offline conversations.

Activist Approach

Some people are inspired by the rallying cry of "Come out, come out, wherever you are." These folks see coming out as a form of activism and a way to challenge societal norms in a highly public or politicized way. They prefer to come out in a speech, an essay, a media interview, or at a public event. The upsides are putting a human face to LGBTQ identities, furthering visibility, and paving the way for others, but the downsides are opening yourself up to the court of public opinion and becoming a spectacle or spokesperson.

The Never-Really-in Approach

There are also folks, often from younger generations, who never really feel 'in the closet' to begin with. They've grown up in more accepting environments, had openly LGBTQ family or role models, and haven't absorbed as much homophobia, making their identity as gay no longer a revelation or a big deal but rather just a fact of life integrated from an early age. While they may not be out in every single setting, being gay is largely a non-issue. This is a new phenomenon that points to the progress made and the work still left to do.

Ultimately, there's no singular "right" way to come out—only what's right for each individual based on their safety, circumstances, and readiness. You get to come out as swiftly or gradually, publicly or privately, casually or ceremoniously as works for you. The key is to honor your unique process with compassion each step of the way.

At the same time, it's crucial for every gay person to work toward living openly and authentically to the greatest degree by coming out and sharing their stories. Coming out is a radical act of bravery and a potent form of activism just by virtue of being, ensuring the change of hearts, minds, and the world. Each LGBTQ person who lives their truth makes it that much easier for the next. We create change simply by embodying our authentic selves.

Whatever your coming-out path, know that you are part of a lineage of courageous ancestors who fought for the freedom to live and love openly. Every single LGBTQ person today is indebted to the trailblazers who came before us and to the generations who will follow. Coming out is a sacred rite of passage and a key part of the hero's journey as a queer person to reclaim his power, joy, and rightful place in the world, as it just might be the most important thing he ever does.

Benefits of Living Openly and Authentically as a Gay Man

Coming out and living openly as a gay man is not only a courageous, transformative act but also the greatest gift we can give ourselves in terms of mental health, self-esteem, relationships, and overall happiness.

Here's a list of some of the many benefits of living 'out and proud' to help you out:

Improved Mental Health

Hiding such a core part of ourselves as our sexuality is an incredibly heavy burden. It takes immense psychic energy to constantly monitor what we say, how we act, and who we're seen with. This chronic self-editing and secrecy breeds anxiety, depression, shame, and self-loathing. By contrast, coming out releases us from the closet's confines. It allows us to relax, breathe deeply, and simply be ourselves. This brings an immense sense of freedom and peace. It is also endorsed by the research that finds a correlation between higher self-esteem, lower levels of depression and anxiety, and greater life satisfaction overall.

Deeper Relationships

When we're closeted, there's always an invisible barrier between us and others, preventing genuine intimacy and leaving us feeling alone even in the crowd. We can only get so close before bumping up against the secret we're withholding. Coming out allows us to share our full selves with the people we love. It lets them truly know us and frees us up to connect authentically, paving the way for deeper, richer, more satisfying relationships built on honesty and trust. We find that the more we open up, the more others feel safe enough to open up to us in return. Coming out weeds out fair-weather friends and reveals true allies, clearing space for a supportive chosen family.

Finding Community

Living openly as a gay man plugs us into the larger LGBTQ community in a powerful way. We find our people—others who share our experiences, struggles, and triumphs. We have access to a wealth of support, resources, and role models. We discover that we're not alone and that there's a beautiful diversity under the queer umbrella. We have a built-in family and network wherever we go. This sense of belonging and solidarity is incredibly nourishing and vital. It's a salve to the alienation and "only one" syndrome that so many LGBTQ folks face. It reminds us that we're part of an enduring legacy, a social movement, and a sacred lineage of love.

Increased Confidence and Self-Acceptance

Every time we come out, we affirm to ourselves and others that there's nothing wrong with being gay. We chip away at the internalized homophobia that says we're broken and that we're less than. Coming out is a powerful declaration of okayness, a radical act of self-acceptance. It sends the message that we're not ashamed of who we are and that we refuse to hide or apologize for our truth. This boldness has ripple effects across our lives. As our shame shrinks, our confidence and comfort in our own skin grow. We worry less about what others think and become more secure in who we know ourselves to be. This newfound confidence shows up in our careers, our relationships, and our willingness to go after what we want.

Living in Integrity

Coming out allows us to align our inner experience with our outer expression. We no longer have to perform a sanitized version of ourselves or keep track of what we disclose to whom. There's an immense psychic freedom in this congruence. It's hugely enlivening to have our outsides match our insides and to feel a sense of internal and relational integrity. This doesn't mean we have to be out in every single context or divulge the details of our dating lives to strangers. It's about living with an internal sense of wholeness. Being willing to be seen for who we are and having the world meet us there.

Increased Capacity for Joy and Self-Expression

The sheer amount of creative and emotional bandwidth freed up by coming out cannot be overstated. All the energy that goes into self-monitoring and suppression gets liberated for passion, play, risk-taking, and delight. We give ourselves permission to explore and express ourselves more fully—in our style, our career, our relationships, and our self-presentation. We reconnect with pleasure, sensuality, and desire. We are open to all the vibrant shades of the human experience. It's like going from black and white to Technicolor, from a stifling box to a wide-open field. Openly gay poet Mark Doty captures it well: "I felt an overwhelming sense of relief and joyful expansiveness: all that energy I'd put into holding back, lying, pretending, and denying was now available to me for other purposes: for creativity, for building connections with others, for exploring the world."

Dating and Relationship Possibilities

It goes without saying that coming out enormously expands who we can date, fall in love with, and build a life with. While some people manage same-sex relationships in the closet, it's not a context that fosters trust, intimacy, or longevity. It's hard to nurture love in the dark. Coming out allows us to openly seek partners and bring them into our lives in an integrated way. No more secret rendezvous, hidden love letters, or pretending to be "roommates." We're free to hold hands in public, post a couple of photos, and get married. We can build the honest, reciprocal, and enduring gay love that's essential to our well-being.

Being a Role Model

Every single LGBTQ person becomes a role model just by living their truth. We never know who we might inspire—the lonely gay teen, the curious college student, the middle-aged father wrestling with his sexuality. By being visible and embracing our identities, we make it easier for the next person to come out by giving them permission to do the same. Think of the gay public figures you looked up to when you were first coming out—Ellen, RuPaul, your gay uncle. They made it okay to be who you are. Now you get to pay that gift forward by being the representation you wish you saw to make the world a little safer and a little better, just by being boldly and unapologetically yourself.

Living a Purpose-Driven Life

It goes without saying that this is a path that comes with challenges of its own; therefore, thrusting into a social justice movement, whether we sign up for it or not, is one of the challenges that we should be prepared for. This larger sense of purpose and responsibility can be incredibly meaningful and motivating if we recognize that our liberation is bound up with the liberation of all marginalized people. We become part of bending the arc of history toward justice by snapping out of complacency and self-centeredness and by plugging ourselves into something greater than ourselves. This doesn't mean that we have to be on the front lines of activism, though that would be wonderful if you did. It means living with an awareness of our hard-won freedoms and doing what we can to pay them forward. Mentoring LGBTQ youth, coming out in the workplace, supporting queer art, voting like our rights depend on it—because they do. When we live out and are proud, our very being becomes a form of activism.

The benefits of coming out are vast and varied. But they all boil down to one essential thing—the ability to live as our full, authentic selves. The freedom and integrity that come from alignment between our inner and outer realities. The joy and meaning that flow from embracing all parts of who we are.

Wherever you are on the coming-out journey, know that a life of openness and authenticity is available to you. You are entitled to take up space, to be seen, and to be celebrated for exactly who you are. No more shrinking, hiding, or apologizing. The world needs your unique gay light.

Coming out can be terrifying. It takes courage to reveal our tender truths and to risk rejection from those we love most. But it's also the adventure of a lifetime, an act of daring greatly, of betting on ourselves, of leaping into the unknown, and of trusting that we'll fly free.

On the other side, coming out is more aliveness, connection, and peace than you can possibly imagine. There's a reason "coming out" and "coming home" are so often used interchangeably, as they both describe a profound return to self, a reunion with our deepest nature. When we come out, we cross the threshold into our most vibrant, powerful, and purposeful lives. We meet ourselves as if for the first time.

If you are to take one thing from this chapter, let it be the realization that you are so brave, so resilient, and so worthy of everything you desire. Know that you are not alone but a part of a beautiful queer family, and that every time you shine your light, you make it easier for another to do the same. Never underestimate the power of living your truth. It just might change the world.

Navigating Family, Friends, and Work After Coming Out

Coming out is a hugely liberating experience. But it also marks the beginning of a new chapter—one in which we have to navigate our relationships and environments as openly gay men. This can be both exciting and challenging as we integrate our authentic selves into the various spheres of our lives.

Let's look at some common experiences and strategies for navigating the post-coming-out landscape:

Family

For many gay men, family is the hardest place to come out and be out. Since our families have known us the longest and often have the most entrenched expectations of who we're supposed to be. They may have deep-seated religious or cultural beliefs about homosexuality, and the revelation might strike them as a sense of loss, confusion, or fear about what your gayness means for your future and your family.

All of this can make for some rocky initial reactions. Some parents get angry or withdraw, unable to reconcile their vision of you with reality. Some react with denial, insisting it's a phase. Others jump to the worst-case scenarios—you'll never have kids, never be happy, get AIDS, and die alone. And some, if you're very lucky, respond with unconditional love and "What took you so long to tell us?!"

Here is the point where you need to be flexible enough to understand that, regardless of the initial reaction, it's not really about you. Your family members are grappling with their own fears, myths, and grief. They're struggling to shift their heteronormative dreams for you and wrap their heads around a new normal. This doesn't excuse hurtful reactions, but contextualizing them can help us have compassion and patience during a tender time.

Some tips for navigating family post-coming out:

Give it time. Don't measure your family's acceptance by their initial reaction, as it is a process that might take months or even years for them to fully come around. Stay engaged (while protecting your emotional health) and trust that love will help them stretch.

Set clear boundaries. You don't have to tolerate disrespect, harassment, attempts to change you, or endless invasive questioning. Decide what you will and won't put up with, and communicate those lines calmly and clearly. Boundaries are a form of self-love.

Introduce them to your gay world slowly. Invite them to meet your partner, your queer friends, and attend PFLAG meetings. Exposure is a potent antidote to fear. It helps normalize and humanize what may feel foreign or scary.

Provide resources. Buy them a book like "Loving Our Gay Child" or "This is a Book for Parents of Gay Kids." Print out articles that answer common questions. Connect them with other families with LGBTQ kids. Do the emotional labor to help them understand and get comfortable.

Find your chosen family. Create a support network of folks who love and celebrate you unconditionally. Lean on them when the blood family is acting up. Let them help fill any voids, so you're not expecting your family of origin to meet all your needs.

Remember, you've had a lot more time to get used to being gay than they have. Extend some of the grace and patience that you've had to cultivate for yourself. With commitment on both sides and a whole lot of love, many families grow closer than ever post-coming out.

Friends

One of the best parts of coming out is connecting more deeply with friends and finding your squad. You get to bond over shared experiences with queer friends and test the depth and durability of straight friendships. Many gay men are delighted to find that coming out weeds out superficial pals and strengthens their truest connections.

Of course, not every friendship survives the coming-out process. Some straight friends, especially men, may withdraw out of discomfort or unexamined homophobia. There may be some distancing as you enter new social circles and your interests shift. But often, these friendship transitions have a way of making room for new ones that are better fits.

Some tips for navigating friendships after coming out:

- Be yourself, unapologetically. You don't have to perform a palatable or "straight-acting" version of gay. The right friends will love you for you.
- Set boundaries around friendship and attraction. Be clear with straight friends that you're not secretly pining for them, and with gay friends that friendship doesn't equal flirting.
- Be patient with dumb questions. Your friends may need some Queer 101 lessons. Gently educate and redirect when needed.
- Take the lead in calling out homophobia. Set the tone that casual homophobia, even in jest, isn't cool with you. Your friends will follow your cues.
- Bring the worlds together. Integrate your friend groups and help your various circles mingle. Shared activities ease discomfort and help everyone gel.
- Forgive some fumbles. Even the most well-meaning straight friends may say the wrong thing sometimes. Remember intent and give gentle course corrections.

Ultimately, being out sorts your true blue friends from the fair-weather ones. The friends who stick by you and celebrate this new chapter will be priceless companions for the rest of your journey.

Work

The workplace can feel like one of the riskiest places to be, depending on your industry, job security, and office culture. There are still 28 states where you can be legally fired just for being gay. And while progress is being made, many work environments remain casually homophobic, if not outright hostile.

This leaves many gay men feeling stuck between a rock and a hard place—wanting to live authentically but fearing professional consequences. The choice to come out at work is highly individual and warrants careful consideration of your specific circumstances.

Some questions to consider:

- Are there any other openly LGBTQ folks at your workplace? How are they treated?
- Does your company have a non-discrimination policy that includes sexual orientation? Is it enforced?
- What's the culture like? Is it highly professional or emotionally intimate? Conservative or progressive?
- How much do your co-workers share about their personal lives? Is being closeted costing you social capital or career opportunities?
- Do you have job security, savings, or other employment options if things go south?
- What's your personal coming out style—do you prefer to tell people directly or just live openly and let them figure it out? Both are valid.

- What feels worse—the stress of hiding or the stress of potential discrimination?

Again, there's no universally right choice here. Some gay men decide that being closeted at work is an acceptable trade-off for income security and peace of mind. For others, it feels stifling and unsustainable to compartmentalize such a core part of themselves for 40+ hours a week.

Here are some strategies to consider if you plan on coming out at work:

- **Know your rights:** Familiarize yourself with your company's policies and any state laws around discrimination. Document any incidents of harassment or unfair treatment.
- **Consider telling HR first:** In some company cultures, looping in HR before coming out to your team can be a smart move. It alerts them that you're now in a protected class and should be treated accordingly.
- **Start with trusted colleagues:** Test the waters by telling work friends you know will be chill. Let it spread organically, and keep an eye out for any negative reactions you may need to address.
- **Focus on performance:** Some worry that coming out will distract from their professional image. Counter this by keeping the focus on your great work. Make your gayness a non-issue by being so damn good they can't afford to care.
- **Find allies:** Seek out other LGBTQ folks and allies at your company or in your industry. Having a supportive network makes everything easier.

- **Transfer internally:** If your direct team feels unwelcoming, see if there are other departments or locations you could move to while staying at the company. LGBT employee resource groups can help navigate this.
- If your workplace is unsupportive, keep an eye out for more inclusive pastures to go where you're valued. Bear in mind that being out and thriving is the best revenge.

Being out at work isn't always easy, but it comes with some major upsides. For one, it can be a huge relief to not have to hide or self-censor for such a large chunk of your waking hours. It frees up bandwidth to focus on your actual job and development.

It also allows you to bring your full self to work and forge deeper relationships with colleagues. People can tell when you're holding back, and it limits intimacy and trust. Being out unburdens you from keeping track of what you've disclosed or accidentally outing yourself after a few too many happy hours.

Finally, being out at work turns you into an activist and trailblazer, whether you meant to be one or not. You expand people's image of what a gay person looks like. You give clients and co-workers a personal connection to LGBTQ issues. And you make it infinitely easier for the next gay hire to be out from day one.

So much of navigating the world as an openly gay man comes down to this: Deciding what you're willing to risk in the service of showing up fully. In case you happen to choose authenticity over safety, know that you have created a ripple effect of permission that could extend far beyond what you can see.

You never know who you're inspiring to live a little more truthfully, both queer folks and straight ones. The more you step into your truth, the more the world has to stretch to meet you there, making things better for all of us.

Being True to Yourself in Relationships

One of the most profound (and sometimes painful) places we feel the impact of coming out is in our relationships. Being openly gay usually means a major shakeup of our social and romantic lives. As we start living more authentically, our relationships have to shift to accommodate this new, truer version of us, which can be both liberating and disorienting as we navigate uncharted territory with partners, family, friends, and ourselves.

Let's break down what being true to yourself can look like in various relational contexts:

With a Partner

If you come out in the context of a straight relationship, you're likely to face some heavy decisions and conversations. How does your partner fit into this new understanding of yourself? Can the relationship adapt, or is it time to part ways? Is there a scenario where you could openly explore your sexuality while staying together?

Some couples, instead of ending their loving relationship, make a conscious choice to stay together, renegotiate their contract, and find a new way forward. This can look like opening the relationship, planning for co-parenting, or shifting into a deep friendship. The key is radical honesty, frequent communication, and a shared commitment to having everyone's needs met.

If you do decide to end a relationship to explore gay life more fully, be kind to yourself and your partner. Allow space to grieve what you're letting go of, even as you move toward what's calling you. One way you can make the process of coming out easier for yourself and your partner could be to stay as transparent and ethical as possible and also acknowledge that there are chances that you will stay a "bad guy" for your ex-partner for a while.

Moving into the gay dating world can be a thrilling and terrifying prospect after coming out. Suddenly, you have access to all these beautiful men—but you may feel like a teenager starting from scratch. Don't worry; every gay man has been there, struggling to pace themselves. All you need to do is communicate your experience level and not put too much pressure on yourself to "catch up."

Some Tips

- Be upfront about your freshly-out status. This gives your date context for your journey and allows them to meet you where you're at. The right guys will be patient and tender with your "baby gay" self.
- If you're not ready to date, don't force it. Focus on making gay friends, getting comfortable in queer spaces, and enjoying your own company. There's no timeline for finding a partner.
- Learn how to kindly turn down dates and say no to sex you're not ready for; instead, a befitting reply would be, "Thanks; I'm flattered, but no thanks." reminding yourself that you don't owe that guy a thing for offering you a drink.
- Use dating apps wisely. Hookup apps like Grindr can be a great way to explore and fulfill fantasies. But they can also feel

like shooting gay culture from a firehose. Pace yourself and remember that there's a whole wide world beyond the apps.

- Be true to your wants and values. Just like in any relationship, you still get to honor your relational and sexual boundaries and desires and muster up the courage to say 'no' to whatever you aren't ready for.

With Friends

Coming out often means a major shift in our friendships, as we start gravitating more toward the queer community and re-negotiating relationships with straight folks. This can involve some growing pains on both sides as identities bump up against each other and find a new normal.

Some straight friends may feel insecure about their place in your life as you embrace your gayness. They may feel left behind as you make new queer pals or develop new interests. The key is to keep communicating and including them as much as feels good to you. Let them know you still love and need them, even as you expand your circle.

You may also encounter some unexamined homophobia, discomfort, or overcuriosity from previously close friends. Navigate this with compassion but also firmness about your boundaries. You're not responsible for performing or downplaying your gayness so others stay comfortable. Your efforts at staying true to yourself will make the real ones rise to the occasion, and the misaligned ones fall away naturally.

Finally, coming out usually means a beautiful blossoming of friendships with other queer folks. These kindred spirits will be a balm and a joy as you navigate your new normal. Seek them out, treasure them, and let them reflect your fabulousness back to you as you find your way. Make space for the riotous laughter, juicy processing, and 'oh my god, you too?!' realness that is queer friendship. It will feed and sustain you like nothing else.

With Family

Being freshly out with family can feel like navigating a minefield of expectations, projections, and misunderstandings. Every family has its own journey of integrating this new information, and it's rarely a straight line from resistance to acceptance.

The key to staying grounded in your truth and having heaping compassion for yourself is the acknowledgment that you don't have to perform the perfect, sparkly gay son or brother to earn your family's love, nor do you have to tolerate mistreatment, no matter how well-intentioned.

Set clear boundaries around your emotional and physical safety. You get to decide how much of your gay life you share with family and when. You get to tell your grandma to keep her "love the sinner, hate the sin" comments to herself. You get to skip family events that feel toxic and create the holiday rituals that nourish you.

It is equally worthwhile to empathize with your family's process without capitulating to it and remind yourself that they're pushing against a lifetime of conditioning and heteronormative fantasies for you. Giving them resources, exposure to your queer life, and plenty of time to stretch into your new shared reality will go a long way.

And above all, surround yourself with your chosen family, who will celebrate you unconditionally and give you a soft place to land as you navigate the hard stuff back home.

With Yourself

Your relationship with yourself should be the focal point after coming out, as you've just done one of the hardest and bravest things a person can do. You've committed to living in alignment with your deepest truth, no matter the consequences. This sort of radical self-honesty is a muscle that will serve you for life in all your relationships.

Being true to yourself as a newly out gay man means giving yourself bucketloads of grace and patience as you feel your way forward. Your learning curve is steep, and that's okay—take it one breath, one conversation, and one awkward date at a time. Let yourself fumble and make mistakes, and pick yourself back up.

It means celebrating every triumph, every flicker of self-love, and belonging along the way. You are healing ancient wounds and righting generations of wrong with every step you take. Never forget how far you've already come just by embracing your own being.

And it means surrounding yourself with images, experiences, people, and practices that affirm your gorgeous gay self. Find the spaces and faces that make you feel seen, sexy, valued, and loved. Let their mirror strengthen the voice inside that knows how lovable you've always been, just as you are.

The world's story about being gay is still one of struggle, but you get to write a triumphant new ending, starting now. One where being true to yourself isn't a liability but the very key to freedom. Being gay is a gift, an honor, and a sacred responsibility passed down by generations of queer ancestors who gave everything so you could shine.

Today, let's decide to believe that story instead. Let's live its truth so loudly that it drowns out any other version. Let's bring the full height and heat of our hard-won authenticity to every connection and every room we enter. Let's stop auditioning for the love and acceptance that have always been our birthright. Let's fall in love with the face in the mirror and call him home for good.

You, dear one, are a miracle. An improbable, precious, on-purpose spark of creation. And the world needs your exact flame, your one-of-a-kind song, today more than ever. So the next time you're standing at the threshold of a new connection—a fresh start, a chance to show up as you really are—take a deep breath and walk through, trusting that life itself wants to meet you there, in all your magnificent truth.

It turns out that the pot of gold at the end of the rainbow was you all along. So claim your rightful place and your untamable shine. Call yourself beloved, and know down to your bones that you're right and the best is yet to come.

Chapter 3: Building a Support System

The Value of Supportive Friends, Family, and Community

No gay man is an island, and we all need a robust support system to thrive, especially in a world that can still be hostile to our very existence. Having people in our corner who love and affirm us unconditionally is essential to our mental health, self-esteem, and overall well-being. It's the foundation that allows us to weather challenges, celebrate triumphs, and become our best selves.

When we first come out, building this support system can feel daunting. We may have strained relationships with family, a largely straight social circle, and no idea where to find our people. But with intention and courage, every gay man can create the network of support and belonging that we all deserve. It just takes some vulnerability, initiative, and a willingness to seek connection.

Let's break down the value of various types of support and how to cultivate them:

Friends

Friends make up for the family in this time of need, as they are the ones who show up for us day in and day out, through the good, the bad, and the fabulous. Therefore, having a tight-knit circle of friends as a gay man is invaluable for so many reasons:

Shared Understanding

Gay friends just get it. They've been through similar struggles and triumphs, and can offer empathy, advice, and solidarity like no one else. With them, you can let your guard down and be fully seen and understood.

Belonging

Being part of a gay friend group fulfills our deep human need for belonging, as it provides a point of reference and a safe haven where we can be ourselves without fear of judgment or rejection. It's a place to laugh, cry, kiki, and just exhale in the company of people who mirror and celebrate us.

Inspiration

Seeing our gay friends live boldly and authentically gives us permission to do the same. They expand our sense of what's possible and show us different ways to be gay in the world. Their courage and resilience rub off on us, lighting the way forward.

Accountability

True friends hold us accountable to our highest selves by calling us out when we're self-sabotaging or not living our values. They remind us of our worth and potential when we've forgotten by not letting us settle for less than we deserve in life and love.

Fun

Gay friends are the gateway to gay culture and community. They're our wingmen on the dancefloor, our plus-ones to Pride, our partners in crime for all the fabulous adventures that queer life has to offer. Life is just more fun and sparkly with them by our side.

It requires a deliberate effort to build strong, nourishing friendships, which could be time-consuming but worth the effort. You can simply start by getting a clear picture of the kinds of friends you want to attract. Begin by asking yourself what qualities and values are most important to you or what kinds of activities and conversations light you up. Answers to these introspective questions will make it easier for you to find a like-minded circle of friends.

Then, get proactive about putting yourself out there. Join LGBTQ social or sports groups, volunteer for queer organizations, and strike up conversations with cute guys at coffee shops or bookstores. Follow your interests and passions, and trust that your vibe will attract your tribe. The more you show up as yourself, the more aligned friends you'll magnetize.

Be the kind of friend you want to have by reaching out, making plans, asking questions, and listening deeply. Celebrate your friends' wins, have their backs through challenges, and be generous with your time, energy, and resources. It is a two-way street; you can make it more fulfilling by investing yourself in it.

Finally, it is equally recommended to let go of friendships that no longer serve you. As our social needs change, so do our circumstances. It's okay to drift away from people who don't understand or support the man you're becoming. Trust that the right friends will stick by you and cheer you on, no matter what.

Family

Family can be a tricky area for many gay men. Some of us are blessed with parents and siblings who rally around us from day one, showing up to Pride parades and baking rainbow cakes. But for many, family is the last place we feel safe and celebrated for our gayness.

You have to wrap your head around the fact that you deserve to be loved and embraced by your family for being who you are. It is their responsibility to bring themselves to offer that to you; if they can't, their unempathetic behavior or rejection is none of your fault. It means they have some growing to do, and you can only control your side of the street.

If you're struggling with an unsupportive family, here are some tips:

Set Boundaries

You don't have to endure homophobic comments, conversion therapy pressure, or relentless questions about your sex life. Calmly let your family know what you will and won't tolerate, and follow through on those limits.

Give it Time

Remember, you've had a lot longer to adjust to being gay than they have. Give them space to express their reactions and process their feelings. Keep showing up authentically, and trust that love will help them stretch—even if it takes years.

Seek Out Chosen Family

Build a network of LGBTQ elders, mentors, friends, and partners who give you the family experience you crave. Let their love and acceptance be a balm and a blueprint for what's possible. Blood doesn't have a monopoly on family.

Control What You Can

You can't control how your family responds to your gayness, but you can control how much space they take up in your life. Limit contact if needed, seek therapy, and pour your energy into the people and pursuits that light you up.

Forgive, for Your Own Sake

Holding on to anger and resentment only hurts you in the end. Work on forgiving your family for their limitations, even if they never change. This isn't condoning their behavior—it's freeing yourself from the pain of expecting them to be different.

At the same time, don't write off your biological family too quickly, and give them a chance to rise to the occasion and surprise you by inviting them into your world bit by bit—a dinner with your partner, a movie with a gay theme, a hometown Pride event. Let them see up close how happy and whole you are as a gay man.

Many families come around in their own time, as their love for you overshadows their fear and ignorance. They may never be marching beside you at Pride but they can still be valuable supporters and allies on your path. Embrace the ways they are able to show up while continuing to seek support in other places as needed.

Community

Community is where we find our mirrors and our medicine as gay men. It gives you a sense of contentment that you are not alone. There is an LGBTQ community that is there to help you discover a sense of history and lineage, share purpose to sustain you for life, and remind you that you have your people to share joys and struggles. It is where we come to be lifted, celebrated, and challenged to grow.

You will find it surprising to discover different facets of the LGBTW community, such as sports, activism, drag, leather, art, or even spirituality. Under our rainbow umbrella, there are infinite ways to be gay and countless subcultures to explore until you land on your own unique place in the colorful tapestry of LGBTQ diversity.

Some ways to get involved and tap into the gay community are:

LGBTQ Centers

Most cities have an LGBTQ community center that offers events, classes, support groups, health services, and more. It's a great place to meet people, access resources, and plug into your local gay scene.

Pride Events

From giant parade spectacles to intimate open mic nights. Pride season bursts with opportunities to celebrate and connect. Show up, strike up conversations, and let yourself be swept up in the collective joy and resilience of our tribe.

LGBTQ Organizations

There are countless nonprofits and community groups dedicated to various aspects of queer life: sports leagues, choruses, professional networks, spiritual centers, political clubs, support services, and more. Find one that aligns with your interests, and get involved as a member, volunteer, or leader.

Gay Social Events

From dance parties to dinner parties, gay men love to gather and let loose. Seek out events that appeal to you, whether low-key game nights or all-night ragers. Show up open and curious, and trust that your people are waiting to find you too.

Online Communities

In the digital age, the gay community is just a click away. Join LGBTQ Facebook groups, follow queer influencers on Instagram, swipe on Tinder, and dive into gay Reddit threads. Just remember that an online connection is no substitute for in-person contact (and can come with its own pitfalls).

As you explore different pockets of the community, pay attention to where you feel most at home. Where can you exhale, be yourself, and connect authentically to feel energized, validated, and a part of something bigger than yourself? Prioritize those spaces and start forging deeper ties within them.

Don't be afraid to get vulnerable and share your story, struggles, and dreams with your queer peers. Intimacy and trust are built through shared vulnerability. The more real you get, the more opportunity you create for meaningful connection. That guy sitting across from you at the gay book club just might become a lifelong friend—but only if you open up and let him in.

At times, the LGBTQ community can feel fragmented, competitive, or downright catty. We're not immune to the same social ills as the wider world, and internalized homophobia can manifest as nastiness toward each other. Don't let this deter you from seeking connection, but do be discerning about the environments and interactions you engage in. Seek out spaces of solidarity, empowerment, and mutual uplift, and be a force for those values yourself. The way we treat each other is the culture we create together.

Finally, always remember that you have so much to offer the gay community through your unique voice, vision, and gifts to help our collective flourish. Seek support and belonging, but also look for ways to give back and pay it forward by being a mentor, an advocate, and a shoulder to lean on for the next generation. We rise by lifting each other, and that starts with each of us showing up fully.

Supportive friends, family, and community are essential nutrients for any gay man's growth and happiness, but they're not always easy to come by, especially early in our journeys. Commit to building your support system with patience, intention, and self-compassion. Reach out, take risks, and keep showing up as your most authentic self to the people who are out there, waiting to love you and cheer you on. You've got this.

Finding and Making Gay Friends

Ah, gay friendship—one of life's sweetest, most satisfying pleasures. There's just something magical about the bonds we form with other queer men. The shorthand and inside jokes, the shared references and resilience, and the way we witness and hold each other through life's plot twists. Gay friends are the family we choose, the mirrors that affirm us, the partners in crime who make the whole wild ride worthwhile.

But for many of us, especially when we're newly out, finding and making gay friends can feel daunting. We may have grown up with few or no examples of what healthy queer male friendship looks like. We may feel awkward or intimidated trying to break into established gay social circles. Or we may have been burned by gay drama and cattiness in the past and feel reluctant to put ourselves out there again.

Here's the thing: Like any friendship, gay friendship requires vulnerability, effort, and a willingness to show up authentically. It means being proactive about seeking connection, taking social risks, and building intimacy over time. And it means learning to be a good friend to ourselves first, so we can attract and sustain the kinds of relationships we desire.

Ready to expand your gay social circle and find your tribe? Here are some tips and strategies to try:

Put Yourself Out There

The number one key to making gay friends is simply being open and available for connection. This means saying yes to social invitations, striking up conversations with strangers, and being proactive about making plans and initiating hangouts. It means taking chances and risking a little awkwardness or rejection in the name of forging new bonds.

Some specific ways to put yourself out there are:

Attend LGBTQ Events

Show up to Pride festivals, gay bar crawls, queer art shows, drag bingo nights, and beyond. Introduce yourself to people, ask questions, and be open to wherever the night takes you. The more consistently you show up in gay spaces, the more familiar faces you'll start to recognize.

Join Queer Groups and Organizations

Sign up for an LGBTQ sports league, political club, professional network, or interest group. Become a regular at your local gay community center's events and volunteer opportunities. Embed yourself in queer spaces where you can meet people with common passions.

Use the apps (wisely)

Dating and hookup apps like Grindr and Tinder can be a great way to connect with local gay men—not just for romance but for friendship too (Kerlin, 2023). Be upfront in your profile about what you're looking for, and don't be afraid to suggest a platonic hangout with a promising match. Just be discerning and always prioritize your safety.

Throw Your Own Event

Don't you see the kind of gay social gathering you're craving? Create it yourself! Host a queer potluck, book club, crafting circle, or game night. Invite a few gay acquaintances and ask them to bring friends. See this as an opportunity to step into a leadership role and be seen as a connector and magnet for new relationships.

Putting yourself out there also means letting your guard down and allowing yourself to be seen and known as someone who is proud to share his story, struggles, and authentic self—even when it feels vulnerable. The deeper you're willing to go with others, the deeper the friendship potential.

Follow Your Authentic Interests

A key to finding your gay friend group is to engage in activities and environments that genuinely light you up. Rather than contorting yourself to fit into a scene that's not really you, follow your natural passions and curiosities. Chances are high that you'll meet compatible friends along the way.

So if you're a gay outdoorsman, join a queer hiking club. If you're a movie buff, start a gay film society. If you're a budding yogi, hit up an LGBTQ yoga retreat. Let your true interests be your guide, and trust that your people will appear in those spaces.

This is also a great way to expand your gay social circle beyond the usual suspects. If all your gay friends are club kids you met at the bars, you might crave some variety. Branching out into different activities and subcultures can introduce you to a whole new crop of potential pals.

Following your authentic interests also makes you a more attractive friend. When we're lit up by something, our enthusiasm and joy are contagious. We attract others who share our passion or who are drawn to our unique energy. By geeking out on what you love and sharing it with others, you become a magnet for meaningful connection.

Be a Good Friend to Yourself

Building a strong relationship with yourself and self-acceptance goes a long way toward building strong friendships with others.

When we're judging, neglecting, or abandoning ourselves, we unconsciously invite others to do the same. But when we treat ourselves with compassion, respect, and appreciation, we attract friends who mirror that back to us.

One of the best things you can do to find quality gay friends is to be a good friend to yourself. This means:

Practicing Self-Compassion

Be kind and patient with yourself as you navigate the ups and downs of gay socializing. Don't beat yourself up for awkward moments or perceived rejections. Treat yourself like you would a dear friend—with gentleness, understanding, and encouragement.

Setting Healthy Boundaries

Know your limits and honor them, even in the face of peer pressure or FOMO. No one will respect your choices unless you do. Don't hesitate to say yes to hangouts or activities that feel draining or inauthentic to you.

Cultivating Self-Love

Treat yourself to regular acts of self-care, celebration, and indulgence by prioritizing your own needs and desires, and by giving yourself permission to invest in your happiness. The more you love and value yourself, the more you magnetize friends who do the same.

Communicating Authentically

Be honest and direct in expressing your thoughts, feelings, and needs. Don't expect others to read your mind or silently resent them when they can't. The more you model authentic communication, the richer and more fulfilling your friendships will be. Remember, attracting amazing friends starts with being an amazing friend to ourselves. By treating ourselves with love, respect, and integrity, we set the stage for relationships that reflect our worth.

Let Go of Unhealthy Attachments

Sometimes, the key to finding our true gay friendships is letting go of the ones that no longer fit. As we grow and evolve, our social needs and compatibilities can shift. Friendships that once sustained us may start to feel draining, toxic, or just plain stale. That's okay—it's a natural part of outgrowing old dynamics and making space for new ones.

If you find yourself in an unhealthy gay friendship that's no longer serving you, don't be afraid to distance yourself or set firmer boundaries. This might mean:

- Saying no to invitations that feel obligatory or depleting.
- Interrupting gossip, cattiness, or shit-talking and redirecting the conversation.
- Calling out behavior that feels unkind or out of integrity.
- Expressing your needs and feelings directly, even when it's uncomfortable.
- Taking space from the friendship to reevaluate its role in your life.

Remember, ending or de-prioritizing a friendship doesn't make you a bad person. It's a sign of self-respect and growth. By letting go of dynamics that drain you, you create space for relationships that truly see and support the man you're becoming. You teach people how to treat you based on what you're willing to accept. Raising the bar and requiring mutuality and respect is a powerful act of self-love.

The friends who are meant to go the distance with you will rise to the occasion and cheer you on as you grow. They'll take accountability for their own baggage and bad habits and be willing to have the tough conversations necessary to get your connection back on track, but it’s okay to let them go if they're not able to meet you where you're at. Send them love and release them to make room for the new soul-nourishing friendships just over the horizon. Trust that as you keep walking with integrity, your tribe will find you.

Joining LGBT Organizations and Support Groups

The gay journey can be unnerving, which could be made easier by building a strong support system through involvement with LGBT organizations and groups that resonate with your interests, skills, or background. These are spaces specifically created by and for our community where we can find belonging, resources, and opportunities to make a difference.

The beauty of LGBT organizations is their incredible diversity. Under the rainbow umbrella, you'll find groups dedicated to every facet of queer life imaginable—from sports teams to spiritual centers, political clubs to professional networks, theater troupes to support groups, and beyond—offering a unique way to connect with like-minded folks, develop your passions, and contribute to the greater good.

Let's explore some of the most common types of LGBT organizations and how they can support your growth and happiness as a gay man:

Community Centers

Most major cities (and many smaller towns) have an LGBT community center that serves as a hub of resources, events, and programs. These centers are often the first stop for folks seeking support, connection, and info on all things queer, offering a wide range of services such as:

- Social events and meetups
- Support groups and counseling
- Health services like HIV testing and PrEP
- Arts and cultural programs
- Youth and senior services
- Legal aid and advocacy

You can always plug into your community, access support, and give feedback by getting involved with your local LGBT center. You might attend a few events as a participant, then volunteer for a program that speaks to you. Many centers have opportunities to lead groups, organize events, or join the board. The more you show up and lend your talents, the more fulfillment and connection you'll find.

Political and Advocacy Groups

For many gay men, part of building a support network means fighting for our rights and working toward a more just world. LGBT political and advocacy groups offer a powerful way to channel our passion into concrete change, amplify our voices, and have a real impact on life-shaping policies and attitudes by joining forces with others.

Some well-known LGBT advocacy groups include:

Human Rights Campaign (HRC)

The largest LGBT civil rights organization in the U.S. is fighting for legal and lived equality through lobbying, education, and political action (NALP, n.d.).

GLAAD

Works to combat anti-LGBT discrimination and accelerate acceptance through media monitoring, education, and celebrity engagement (Schifter, 2021).

Lambda Legal

The oldest and largest legal organization dedicated to achieving full civil rights for LGBT people through litigation and public policy work (Lambdalegal, n.d.).

Victory Fund

Trains, supports, and advocates for openly LGBT candidates running for public office at all levels of government (Victoryfund.org, 2019).

There are various ways in which you can get involved with an LGBT political group, depending on whether you want to keep things easy or go deeper. Some of the simple ways could be such as attending a rally, donating money, or writing to your representatives about an issue. On a deeper level, you can volunteer for a campaign, join a committee, or even run for office yourself. Political activism will serve you twofold: By providing you with a platform to socialize and by bringing about concrete change.

Social and Recreational Groups

Not every LGBT group has to be serious business. In fact, some of the most nourishing support comes from the fun, lighthearted connections we make through shared hobbies and interests. One great way to make friends, blow off steam, and just feel at home in your own skin is to join such social and recreational queer groups.

Some popular types of LGBT social groups include:

It's a great way to stay active, make friends, and represent your community on the field or court by joining sports leagues such as softball, soccer, swimming, and skiing. You can even join LGBT amateur sports leagues in most major cities.

Interest Clubs

Into reading, hiking, cooking, or crafting? Chances are high that there's a gay group for that. Sites like Meetup and Facebook are great for finding niche communities of queer folks who geek out on the same things you do.

Party Promoters

If you're more of a "see and be seen" type, get on the list for your local gay party promoters and event producers. From giant circuit parties to intimate cocktail soirées, these gatherings are prime places to dance, flirt, and expand your social circle. Just remember to party responsibly.

Dinner Clubs

For the foodies out there, gay dinner clubs are a delicious way to break bread and build community. Members often take turns hosting themed meals at home or meet up to try new restaurants together. Bon appetit!

The key to finding the right social group is to follow your bliss. Explore the gay scenes that genuinely light you up, whether that's a drag queen book club or an LGBT rock climbing crew. The more you align with your authentic interests, the more compatible friends you'll naturally attract.

Support and Discussion Groups

Sometimes, the most valuable support we can find is simply being in a room with others who get it. LGBT support and discussion groups offer a confidential space to share our stories, struggles, and triumphs with peers who've been there. By witnessing each other and holding on to each other, we remind ourselves that we're not alone.

Common types of LGBT support groups include:

- For folks at all stages of the coming-out process, these groups provide guidance, encouragement, and community during a vulnerable time.

- For gay men living with HIV, these groups offer a safe space to talk about the unique challenges and joys of life with the virus. From discussing medication side effects to navigating dating and disclosure, no topic is off limits.
- Gay men face higher rates of substance abuse, often as a way to cope with minority stress and trauma. LGBT-specific 12 step meetings and recovery groups provide a crucial lifeline and fellowship for those seeking sobriety.
- Depression, anxiety, and other mental health challenges are sadly all too common in our community. LGBT therapy groups and peer support circles remind us that we don't have to struggle alone.
- For queer folks seeking to reconcile their sexuality with their religious or spiritual beliefs, these groups offer a welcoming space to explore the intersection of identities. From inclusive churches to Buddhist sanghas, there's a faith community for everyone.

One of the most revolutionary things about LGBT support groups is the way they normalize and validate our experiences by hearing our struggles echoed in the stories of others. We come to see our pain not as a personal failure but as a shared struggle rooted in systemic oppression, which could be incredibly liberating and empowering. Some people prefer to process privately or one-on-one with a therapist, which is okay as support groups aren't for everyone. But if you are struggling, consider giving a group a try; as for many gay men, the experience of being seen and supported by a room full of peers is life-changing. You might be surprised by the strength and solidarity you find.

Professional Networks

Our professional lives are one of the most important arenas for building support and advancing equality as gay men. By connecting with other LGBT folks in our industries, we tap into a powerful network of mentors, collaborators, and changemakers. We also pave the way for greater visibility, inclusion, and allyship in the workplace.

Most major professional fields have an LGBT networking organization, from finance to tech to law to academia. Groups like Out in STEM, the National LGBT Bar Association, and Out Professionals offer conferences, mentorship programs, job boards, and leadership development for rising queer talent. By getting involved, you gain access to invaluable career resources and relationships.

LGBT professional groups also provide a space to strategize around the unique challenges we face in the workplace, such as coming out to colleagues, navigating office politics as a minority, and advocating for inclusive policies. By sharing our experiences and success stories, we equip each other to thrive and drive change in our fields.

Even if you're not actively job-seeking, engaging with an LGBT professional network keeps you plugged into industry trends and expands your social capital. The connections you make could lead to exciting opportunities down the road or just a new friendship with someone who shares your passions. Plus, it feels damn good to bring your full authentic self to your work life and be celebrated for it.

Arts and Cultural Groups

For centuries, LGBT people have found community and expression through the arts. From the gender-bending stars of Vaudeville to the trailblazing talents of New Queer Cinema, we've long used creativity as a tool for visibility, protest, and social change, and these days, queer arts and culture are more vibrant than ever, with countless ways to get involved.

Some common LGBT arts groups include:

Community Choirs and Bands

Raise your voice for equality (literally) by joining an LGBT choir, orchestra, or marching band. The sense of harmony and belonging is unbeatable.

Theater and Improve Troupes

Channel your inner diva and find your chosen family onstage. LGBT theater companies mount everything from campy musicals to searing dramas, often highlighting queer stories and artists.

Film Festivals and Media Groups

Some other ways to connect and get an insider's look into queer culture storytelling are by volunteering for an LGBT film festival, joining a queer filmmaking collective, or writing for an LGBT publication.

Drag and Nightlife Collectives

If you are a performer and a party monster, you can experience a glittery gateway to friendship, creative fulfillment, and killer looks by getting involved with your local drag scene or queer nightlife community.

Participating in LGBT arts and culture is a joyful reminder that we are a people with a rich history and a boundless capacity for beauty. By uplifting queer creators and preserving our cultural legacy, we strengthen our sense of pride, and resilience in the face of adversity. We also just have a damn good time expressing ourselves and appreciating each other's talents.

No matter what kind of LGBT organization speaks to you, the key is to show up and keep showing up. Building real relationships and support networks takes consistency and vulnerability. It means daring to let yourself be seen, getting curious about others' stories, and being generous with your own gifts for developing friendships and belonging.

This doesn't necessarily mean that you have to join every LGBT group out there to reap the benefits. You can simply start with one or two that genuinely excite you and give yourself permission to explore at your own pace. Trust that the right people and opportunities will find you when you pursue what lights you up.

At the end of the day, getting involved with LGBT organizations isn't just about what you gain individually; rather, it's about taking part in something greater than yourself, such as strengthening the social fabric that sustains us all as queer people. By showing up for your community, you create a ripple effect of support, visibility, and change that touches lives beyond your own and creates a legacy.

Being a Support for Other Gay Men

One of the most rewarding parts of building a strong support network is getting to pass it on to others. It provides us with a unique opportunity and a sense of responsibility to be available to the brothers who are still struggling with this newly acquired identity by offering our hard-won wisdom, empathy, and encouragement.

Being a supporter of other gay men doesn't have to be a grand or formal gesture; rather, small acts of kindness and connection add up to a stronger, more resilient community for us all. You can be supportive by simply striking up a conversation with a shy guy at a party, offering to grab coffee with a friend going through a tough breakup, or sending an encouraging text to a buckle-up colleague.

Of course, being truly supportive does require a certain degree of emotional intelligence, maturity, and follow-through. Here are some key qualities and skills to cultivate as you strive to be a pillar for your gay brothers:

Empathetic Listening

One of the greatest gifts we can give another person is our full, undivided attention when a gay friend or acquaintance trusts us enough to share their story or struggle. We can win their trust by simply listening to them with an open heart. This means:

- Putting away distractions like phones and really focusing on the person in front of you.
- Resisting the urge to interject with your own anecdotes or advice right away.

- Asking thoughtful questions will draw them out and show you're engaged.
- Reflecting back on what you hear will make sure you're understanding correctly.
- Validating their emotions and experiences, even if you haven't been through the same thing.

The goal isn't to fix their problems or have all the answers but to create a safe, non-judgmental space for them to feel seen and heard. Often, just feeling truly listened to can be incredibly healing and empowering for someone going through a hard time.

Skillful Advice-Giving

Once you've fully heard someone out, there may come a point where they explicitly ask for your advice or input. In such a scenario, share your perspective thoughtfully and tactfully whenever such an opportunity arrives. This means:

- Acknowledging that you don't have all the answers and can only speak from your own experience.
- Asking permission before offering suggestions or feedback and respecting their response.
- Focusing on their needs and goals, not just what worked for you in the past.
- Offering advice as possibilities and options, not orders or ultimatums.
- Empowering them to trust their own judgment and make their own choices in the end.

Remember that your job is to keep showing up and cheering them on, and understand that what looks like the obvious right path to you may not be right for them. Everyone has their own journey and timeline. The best thing you can do is offer your honest perspective, then step back and trust their process. They may take your advice, or they may go in a totally different direction.

Healthy Boundaries

To be a sustainable support system for others, we have to get good at recognizing and respecting our own limits. This means being honest about our capacity, energy, and expertise and communicating those boundaries clearly and kindly. It's okay (and necessary) to say things like:

- "I care about you and want to support you, but I'm not qualified to give medical, legal, or financial advice. Let's brainstorm some professionals you could talk to."
- "I've loved being your sounding board these past few weeks, but I'm feeling a bit overextended right now. Could we try meeting up a little less often? I want to make sure I can really show up for you."
- "I know we've been flirty in the past, but now that we're becoming real friends, I want to make sure we're on the same page, and this is platonic. I really value our friendship and don't want to blur any lines."

Setting clear boundaries isn't selfish—it's a way of honoring our needs and protecting the integrity of our relationships. It ensures that we can keep showing up as our best, most grounded selves in the long run. True friends will respect and appreciate our honesty.

Leading by Example

One of the most remarkable ways to live an authentic life is to live by the truth with grace, and we can lead and support other gay men by presenting our life as role models for self-love, personal growth, and community engagement. Our leadership inspires others to do the same.

This means continually doing our own work to heal past wounds, examine our biases, and become the best versions of ourselves by treating ourselves and others with the same compassion, respect, and integrity we wish to see in the world. And it means staying humble and open to learning from every person and experience we encounter.

You have to bear in mind that it's okay if you haven't figured it all out. By staying committed to our own growth and leading with vulnerability, we create a culture of mutual support and evolution in the gay community, which cannot survive if we aren't willing to keep showing up and lifting each other up, as we are all works in progress.

Concrete Ways to Show Support

So, what does being supportive actually look like in practice? Here are some concrete ways to show up for your gay brothers:

- Check in regularly with friends going through a tough time. A simple "How are you holding up?" text can mean the world.
- Offer to accompany a friend to a scary doctor's appointment, a coming-out conversation, or the first gay bar outing, as your presence can be a game-changer.

- Connect friends to helpful resources like therapists, support groups, career mentors, or LGBTQ-friendly service providers. Your Rolodex is a gift.
- Invite a newly single friend to be your plus-one to a party or wedding. Being included in couple-centric spaces can ease the sting of heartbreak.
- Help a friend revamp his dating app profile or choose outfits for a big interview. A little brotherly advice can boost confidence big-time.
- Organize a fundraiser or meal train for a community member going through illness or hardship. A show of practical support reminds them they're not alone.
- Call out casual homophobia or racism when you hear it, even if there are no gay people in the room. Being an ally all the time is how we change hearts and minds.
- Share your story and struggles openly so others feel safe doing the same. Vulnerability begets vulnerability and heals shame in the light of connection.
- Celebrate your friends' milestones and victories like they're your own. Pride is contagious, and life is too short not to toast each other's triumphs.

At the end of the day, your presence means that you are supporting other gay men by showing up and letting love lead the way. You have the responsibility to extend the same grace and generosity to others that we want for ourselves and accept the fact that we belong to each other, and we're stronger when we have each other's backs.

Chapter 4:

Dating and Relationships

Challenges and Opportunities in Gay Dating

Gay dating can be a maddening, exhilarating, and utterly confounding adventure all at once. Few topics elicit as many groans, giddy squeals, and late-night group chats as this perennial roller coaster ride. For gay men, the dating landscape often feels like an endless series of hurdles, heartbreaks, and humorous mishaps—interspersed with those rare, glittering moments of genuine connection and swoon-worthy romance.

You will find it quite surprising that dating as a gay man also presents a unique set of opportunities for growth, self-discovery, and fulfillment. By embracing the challenges and learning to navigate them with humor, heart, and a hefty dose of self-love, we can transform our love lives into a truly empowering and joyful part of our journey. Let's dive into some of the most common challenges gay men face in dating and how to alchemize them into golden opportunities for connection and happiness.

Challenge #1: A Limited Dating Pool

The smaller size of our dating pool than that of our heterosexual counterparts is the obvious challenge of gay dating due to the comparatively smaller gay community. Gay men still make up a tiny fraction of the overall population despite the fact that stigma and discrimination have decreased in recent years. Depending on where you live, it can feel like you've already dated every eligible gay bachelor in town twice.

There are often segregated subgroups based on age, race, body type, HIV status, and gender expression within the gay community that further narrow down one's potential matches. Racism, ageism, ableism, and transphobia abound on gay dating apps and social scenes, as well as dilemmas as to whom we consider viable partners and who considers us.

We can turn this challenge into an opportunity by getting creative, proactive, and intentional about expanding our dating pool and diversifying our approach to meeting people. This might mean:

- Exploring new social scenes and groups outside our usual go-to's by attending a queer book club, joining an LGBT sports league, or volunteering for a cause you believe in. You will encounter more fresh faces through exploring more diverse interests and activities.
- Questioning and dismantling your own "preferences" and biases when it comes to age, race, disability, etc., in partners. Examine where these preferences come from and whether they're closing you off to great guys. Purposefully seek out media, friendships, and spaces that celebrate the full diversity of gay men.
- Redefining what "dating" and "relationship material" mean to you. Does someone have to tick every box to be worth knowing? Can you be open to the magic of connection in unexpected places or people?

- Expanding your geographic radius. It is understood that a small town might offer limited opportunity to find the best partner. One way of dealing with the situation could be to expand your geographic radius by driving an hour to the nearest gayborhood or planning a trip to a city with a vibrant LGBT scene. Besides, dating apps also let you peruse profiles in other places before you travel.
- You can tap into your network by letting your friends and family know you're open to being set up or introduced to potential matches. Your loved ones likely have single gay men in their orbit who could be a great fit for you.

Challenge #2: Hookup Culture

Let's face it: Gay male culture tends to place a big premium on sex and hookups over relationships and romance. Open Grindr on any given night, and you'll be barraged with enough unsolicited close-ups of male anatomy to make even the most sex-positive among us blush. Sex is often treated as the default starting place for connection rather than a precious intimacy to be built up over time.

This hookup-centric culture can pose a real challenge for gay men looking for something more substantial than a one-night stand or FWB situation. It can be tough to discern who's open to a relationship, sort through all the mixed messages and mind games, and build authentic intimacy in an ocean of casual sex and disposable connections.

There is nothing inherently wrong with hookups if that's what you're looking for; an over-emphasis on sex often comes at the cost of other forms of closeness like emotional vulnerability, friendship, coadventuring, and cozy domesticity. Many gay relationships skip over these crucial building blocks of intimacy altogether.

So how do we swim against this tide and create opportunities for the kind of romance we really want? A few ideas include being upfront about what you're looking for in your dating profiles, conversations, and general energy and clearly communicating that you're ultimately seeking a relationship (if that's true for you). Don't be afraid to turn down invitations and advances that don't align with your relationship goals.

Prioritize dates and hangouts that allow you to really get to know each other, such as meeting for coffee or lunch, where you can have a real conversation, take a hike, or attend a cultural event together. Focusing on activities that give you a chance to glimpse each other's minds, hearts, and values will help you find your kind of partner.

Take things slow(er) physically, as there's no need to rush into sex before you feel a solid foundation of trust and care. Enjoy the delicious tension and anticipation of a gradual buildup and savor all the other kinds of intimacy along the way—the long talks, the tender touches, the inside jokes.

Don't put all your eggs in one basket until you've had a clear conversation about exclusivity; just assume the guy you're dating is also seeing other people, and keep your options open too. This helps take the pressure off and keeps you from getting prematurely attached.

Cultivate a strong sense of self-worth and self-sufficiency and acknowledge that you are a complete, lovable person, with or without a partner. Fill your life with passion, purpose, and platonic intimacy so you're not relying on dating to meet all your needs. The fuller your life, the healthier and more discerning you'll be in romance.

Challenge #3: Ambiguous Intentions and Commitment

Gay-male relationships often suffer from a lack of clarity around intentions, expectations, and commitment. Without many models for long-term gay partnerships, and in a dating culture that emphasizes sex and novelty over commitment and continuity, it can be difficult to know if you're on the same page about where things are going.

Sometimes what happens is the difference in expectations from the relationship. For example, you might assume that after a few months of dating, you're well on your way to boyfriendhood—only to be blindsided when he tells you he's not looking for anything serious. Or you find yourself in a quasi-situation that's not quite a relationship but more than a hookup, with no clear direction forward. The ambiguity can be crazy-making.

Gays also have fewer cultural scripts and rituals to mark the progression and solidification of our relationships. There's no engagement party, no wedding, and no established timeline for moving in together or having kids. While this is liberating in many ways, it also means we have to be much more proactive and intentional about having Big Talks and creating our own milestones.

Here are some ways to bring more clarity and commitment to your dating life:

First, clear your head on what you want through journaling, reflection, and getting therapy. Do whatever you need to do to crystallize your own desires and values when it comes to dating and relationships and to clearly communicate with your partner about the needs and expectations of the relationship.

Second, as the relationship progresses, have intentional conversations early and often about your visions and goals, your expectations around sex and exclusivity, your fears, and deal breakers. Set aside time to really hear each other and get on the same page. Yes, these chats can be awkward—do them anyway.

Third, avoid the assumption that you've been dating for a while or met each other's friends, which necessarily means you're in a capital-R relationship. Never assume a certain level of commitment until you've explicitly discussed and agreed to it together.

Fourth, move at a pace that feels good to both of you since there's no one timeline for when different relationship milestones should happen. What matters is that you're both enthusiastic about the pace and trajectory of your connection. If one of you wants to hit the gas while the other has cold feet, you likely have a compatibility issue to sort out.

Fifth, create your own rituals and ways of honoring your love and come up with your own markers of commitment and celebration, whether it's a special piece of jewelry, a private couple's ritual, or an annual adventure. Get creative about making your love feel sacred and tended to, even without society's stamp of approval.

Challenge #4: Internalized Shame and Homophobia

It is natural for us to carry the baggage of shame and guilt from growing up in a homophobic society, which becomes the biggest obstacle to happy and healthy gay relationships. Even if we've done a lot of personal growth work and have a strong sense of gay pride, most of us still have pockets of shame, low self-worth, and internalized stigma about our sexuality and lovability.

This shows up in our dating lives in all sorts of ways: choosing partners who mistreat us because we don't believe we deserve better; shying away from emotional intimacy because we fear authentic connection; dating compulsively to distract from loneliness and existential pain; projecting old familial wounds onto our partner; and repeating unhealthy dynamics from childhood.

Until we do the inner work to address our core shame and insecurities, we'll keep bumping up against the same self-sabotaging patterns in relationships. We've got to re-parent and re-partner ourselves from the inside out, learning to love and nurture the very parts we've disowned.

Some ways to alchemize your shame into dating gold:

You can do your own trauma and inner child work by seeking therapy, joining a men's group, and attending personal growth workshops. You will have more capacity for healthy gay love if you let your wounds and attachment injuries heal early.

Identify your triggers and coping patterns by identifying if having a tough conversation with your dad makes you pick fights with your boyfriend. Does feeling rejected result in a grindr spiral? Notice these patterns with compassion, so you can intervene more skillfully.

Examine your beliefs about what you deserve in love and challenge any narratives you hold about being unlovable, too much, or not enough. Affirm your inherent worthiness of care and respect—then back it up with your dating choices.

Build a strong friendship with yourself. It is pertinent to treat yourself with the same kindness, patience, and affection you would a dear friend by taking yourself on dates, giving yourself pep talks, and celebrating your wins. Reparent the gay boy within until he knows he's precious.

Surround yourself with positive gay role models by seeking out images, stories, and real-life examples of joyful, committed gay love. Let them be a north star for what's possible as you shape your own love story.

The greatest opportunity in gay dating is the chance to finally give and receive the deep intimacy and affection we may have been missing for much of our lives. Each challenge invites us to grow into the confident, open-hearted men we want to be and attract the nourishing love we so richly deserve.

Meeting Potential Partners

So now that we've covered some of the common challenges and opportunities in gay dating let's get into the juicy stuff, such as how to actually meet guys! While the gay dating landscape has certainly changed over the years (hello, apps), there are still tried-and-true ways to connect with new potential partners. Following are some of the best places and strategies for meeting quality men:

Gay Dating Apps

Many of us might have reservations about dating apps, but it goes without saying that whether you love 'em or hate 'em, dating apps have become a staple of modern gay romance. A whopping 80% of gay men use digital dating platforms, such as Grindr and Scruff

(Thomas, 2023). While these apps often get a bad rap for fueling hookup culture and superficial interactions, they can also be a powerful tool for meeting a wide range of guys you might never encounter IRL.

Some tips for using gay apps effectively:

Firstly, fill out your profile thoughtfully and use recent, clear photos that show your face and a bit of your personality/interests. Write a short bio that conveys who you are and what you're looking for, whether that's a LTR, casual dates, or new buddies to explore the city with.

Secondly, be proactive but not pushy. Just don't wait for messages to roll in—scan profiles actively and reach out to guys who intrigue you. At the same time, take a hint if someone isn't responsive or reciprocating your interest. A simple "Hey, how's your week going?" is enough to kick things off.

Thirdly, move the conversation off the app, once you've established a bit of rapport and interest (this can take anywhere from a few messages to a few days, depending on your texting style). Suggest moving to text, a phone call, or an in-person meetup. Lingering in app-land for too long can lead to dead-end pen pals.

Fourthly, be safe and protect your privacy, and never feel pressured to share personal info like your address or phone number before you're ready. If you decide to hook up, always meet in public first and let a friend know your whereabouts. Listen to your gut and cut off contact if you ever feel uncomfortable or unsafe.

Remember, apps are just a tool for introduction—the real magic happens when you take things offline. Treat your profile and online interactions as just the first step towards a face-to-face connection, and don't get too bogged down by the inevitable flakes and fizzles. Stay positive and trust that, with consistent effort, your Prince Charming will eventually grace your grid.

LGBTQ Spaces and Events

While gay bars and clubs have long been go-to spots for meeting potential dates, there are so many other places in the broader LGBTQ community to mix and mingle with quality guys. By getting involved with queer groups and activities that align with your interests and values, you're much more likely to connect with someone compatible than a 2 a.m. bar crush.

Some great places to meet dateable gays could be LGBTQ community centers, as they often host regular mixers, speed dating nights, discussion groups, and social activities designed specifically for singles. It is pretty convenient too; all you need to do is check out the calendar at your nearest center and show up ready to charm.

You can also socialize at pride festivals, parades, and parties, which bring the whole queer community out to play. Strike up a conversation with the cutie next to you as you fight for beads or groove to the DJ. The collective joy and liberation make Pride events an extra flirty and fun place to meet guys.

There is also an opportunity to find a good partner when you join LGBTQ sports leagues such as gay softball. Queer climbing clubs are a fantastic way to meet fit, fun guys who share your passion for getting sweaty, as teamwork and friendly competition make a great jumping-off point for romance.

Queer arts and cultural events like film festivals, drag shows, theater productions, and gallery openings draw a diverse crowd of gay guys who appreciate creativity, and there is a great chance for you to bond over the latest indie gay romcom or sickening lip sync, then invite him to dissect it over a drink.

Most people consider LGBTQ networking and professional groups nothing more than an activity for climbing the career ladder—they can be great places to find an ambitious, put-together man who shares your industry and interests. Many have regular social events and happy hours where you can mix business with a little flirtatious pleasure.

Lastly, Gay travel and tourism, whether it's an all-gay cruise, a queer history walking tour, or an LGBT camping trip, can be a fun and novel way to meet guys from all over. Exploring a new place or experience will create instant camaraderie and lots to talk about. Hence, the key to meeting someone at queer events is to get out of your comfort zone and talk to people! It can be intimidating to fly solo in a sea of gay strangers, but remember that everyone is there to socialize and make new connections. Smile, introduce yourself, ask questions, and offer compliments—be the friendly, approachable guy you'd want to meet. And even if an outing doesn't yield a hot date, treat every new interaction as a chance to practice your flirting skills and expand your social network. You never know who that new gay BFF might introduce you to down the line.

Set-Ups and Fix-Ups

It might be news to you, but it is true that your friends, family, co-workers, and acquaintances collectively know hundreds of gay men—some of whom might be your perfect match—so don't underestimate the power of your existing network when it comes to meeting potential dates. Letting your loved ones know that you're single and open to meeting people can yield some surprisingly great set-ups.

Some ways to work your network for romance include:

- Putting out the word that you're open to fix-ups. You can even do it in a subtle manner by casually mentioning that you're single and looking the next time your coupled-up pals ask about your love life. There is quite a chance that they know a quality guy or two they've been dying to set you up with.
- Consider your extended network, as it's not just your besties who can play matchmaker—your neighbors, yoga teacher, barista, and Instagram followers might also have a single gay friend to introduce you to. Be open about your status in various areas of your life and see what connections come out of the woodwork.
- Give set-ups a real shot. If a friend goes into trouble to fix you up, honor that effort by agreeing to a date and going in with an open mind (assuming you're not getting serial killer vibes). Even if there's no romantic spark, be gracious and use it as a chance to sharpen your dating skills.
- Ask for intel before a set-up. To minimize the awkwardness of a totally blind date, ask your matchmaker friend for some key details about the guy. What does he do for a living? What's his general vibe? What do they think you'll like about him? A little preview can help you relax and plan date talking points.

- Return the matchmaking favor! Playing cupid for your single friends is good dating karma and makes you a valuable resource in your community. Keep an eye out for connections in your circle, and think about who might hit it off. Your intuition and endorsement could help create the next great gay power couple.

At the end of the day, meeting guys IRL is about constantly expanding your network and putting yourself out there as an available, dateable man. The more proactive and open to new people and experiences you are, the more guys you'll meet and the greater your chances of clicking with someone special. Don't just wait for Mr. Right to fall into your lap; go out and find him! Be bold, be curious, and be willing to step outside your comfort zone. Strike up conversations, ask for numbers, and follow up on promising leads. Remember, every "no" or dead end brings you one step closer to a "yes" and a real connection. Trust that your efforts will pay off in due time. And in the meantime, enjoy the thrill of the chase and all the fun, flirty interactions along the way. Embracing the journey of meeting new people is half the battle; the other half is staying open to the possibilities when they present themselves. So keep putting yourself out there, keep honing your dating skills, and keep believing that your perfect match is on his way to you at this very moment. Your next great love story is just waiting to be written.

Developing Healthy Dating and Relationship Skills

Once you've met a promising potential partner (or three), the real work of dating begins. Contrary to rom-com fantasies, healthy relationships don't just happen magically—they take effort, intention, and a whole slew of interpersonal skills that many of us weren't explicitly taught growing up, especially as gay men. The good news is that with practice and perseverance, anyone can become a more emotionally intelligent, communicative, and loving partner. Here are some of the key skills and principles for creating thriving gay relationships:

Honest and Direct Communication

At the foundation of every successful partnership is the ability to express yourself authentically and listen deeply to the other person. This means getting comfortable sharing your true thoughts, feelings, needs, and desires—even when it's scary or uncomfortable. It also means creating a safe space for your partner to do the same without judgment or defensiveness.

Some tips for improving your communication:

- Use "I" statements to express your experience rather than "you" statements that criticize or blame. For example, "I felt hurt when you canceled our date at the last minute" instead of "You're so inconsiderate and flakey."
- Practice active listening by giving your full attention, reflecting back on what you hear, and asking clarifying questions. Resist the urge to interrupt, problem-solve, or react right away.
- Get vulnerable about your fears, insecurities, and dreams. The more you reveal your authentic self, the more your partner can meet you there with empathy and understanding.
- Address conflicts and issues directly and calmly, rather than ignoring them or blowing them up. Schedule intentional time

to talk through challenges and find win-win solutions together.

- Regularly express gratitude and appreciation for the things you love about your partner. Acknowledging the good cultivates more of it!

Emotional Intelligence and Maturity

Gay relationships flourish when both partners have a solid sense of self and can navigate the inevitable ups and downs of intimacy with grace. This means being able to manage your own emotions, tolerate discomfort, apologize and forgive, self-soothe, and find happiness within yourself. In short, grow the eff up.

Some signs of emotional maturity in relationships include the following:

- Taking responsibility for your actions, mistakes, and triggers rather than blaming your partner.
- Allowing your partner to have their own thoughts, feelings, and reactions without trying to control or change them.
- Being able to self-regulate and de-escalate during conflicts rather than adding fuel to the fire.
- Prioritizing the relationship and finding compromise rather than always needing to be "right."
- Knowing how to give and receive love in a way that works for both of you.

If these skills don't come naturally to you, you're not alone. Many of us reached adulthood without learning how to do intimacy well.

The key is committing to your own growth and healing, whether through therapy, self-help books, workshops, or spiritual practice. The more you strengthen your emotional muscles, the easier it will be to show up as a mature, loving partner.

Intentional Dating and Pacing

In the whirlwind of new love, it can be tempting to dive head-first into a relationship and start making all kinds of plans and promises. But taking the time to really get to know someone and assess your compatibility before jumping in full throttle can save a lot of heartache down the road. This is where intentional dating comes in.

Intentional dating means being clear about your values, needs, and desires in a relationship from the start and evaluating potential partners based on how well they align. Rather than getting swept up in chemistry and fantasy, you stay grounded in reality and let things unfold organically, with lots of honest communication along the way.

Some keys to intentional dating:

- Get clear on your core values and dealbreakers before you start dating. What qualities are most important to you in a partner? What dynamics and issues are you unwilling to tolerate?
- Share your relationship desires and expectations early on, ideally before getting sexually involved. Are you looking for something serious or casual? Monogamous or open? Living together or living apart? The earlier you talk about these big issues, the fewer surprises down the road.

- Move at a pace that feels safe and right for both of you. There's no universal timeline for when different relationship milestones should happen. What matters is that you're on the same page, and no one feels rushed or backed into a corner.
- Keep checking in with yourself throughout the dating process. How do you feel in this person's presence? Do you like who you are around them? Is there a good balance of chemistry and compatibility? Paying attention to your gut and your emotional needs will help you make self-honoring choices.
- Don't rush into exclusivity or commitment before you've established a solid foundation of trust, respect, and care. In the meantime, keep your options open, and don't prematurely disqualify other viable partners.

The beauty of intentional dating is that it sets you up for relationship success by ensuring you're diving in with eyes wide open and building on a bedrock of shared values. And if, in the end, you discover you're not a match, you can part ways with clear consciences, knowing you gave it a fair and honest shot.

Interdependence and Maintaining Individuality

One of the greatest joys of a long-term relationship is building a shared life and identity with your partner. Your social circles blend, you co-create a cozy little world, and you become each other's go-to for everything from tough decisions to late-night snacks. But many couples become so enmeshed in couplehood that they lose sight of who they are as individuals, which can breed codependency and dysfunction.

Healthy gay partnerships balance intimacy and autonomy. They cultivate interdependence rather than codependence. Each partner can rely on the other for love and support while still maintaining a solid sense of self and a life outside the relationship. Here are some ways to stay distinct yet deeply bonded:

- Keep pursuing your own passions, friendships, and personal growth. Don't let your hobbies and social life fall by the wayside just because you're together.
- Spend time apart regularly. Take solo trips, have nights out with your own friends, and practice separate self-care. Missing each other is a good thing!
- Maintain financial independence. Even if you share expenses or have joint accounts, make sure you each have funds you control and can spend as you wish.
- Encourage each other's individual dreams and goals, even if they don't always align. Cheer each other on as you chase careers, degrees, and bucket list items.
- Have a rich inner life and ways to emotionally care for yourself. Keep a journal, see a therapist and practice meditation. Fill your own cup so you're not over-relying on your partner for validation and security.
- Respect each other's privacy and personal space. You don't need access to each other's phones, emails, or every waking thought. A little mystery keeps things fresh!

Balancing "I" and "we" isn't always easy, especially if you have an anxious attachment style or a history of unhealthy relationships. It takes trust, security, and good boundaries to let your partner have a separate self without feeling abandoned or betrayed. Keep talking openly about your needs for closeness and space, and be patient with yourselves as you find the right groove.

Sexual Communication and Exploration

Let's be real—one of the major perks of a loving gay relationship is the potential for toe-curling, soul-shaking, next-level sex. When you combine erotic passion with deep emotional intimacy, fireworks tend to follow. But getting there requires being radically honest about your desires, turn-ons, fantasies, and boundaries, which can be scary for a lot of guys.

Contrary to popular belief, mind-blowing sex doesn't just happen spontaneously—it's co-created through courageous communication and uninhibited exploration. Here are some tips for having the gay sex life of your dreams:

- Make talking about sex a regular part of your relationship. Carve out intentional time to share your desires, fantasies, and feedback with each other. Use "I" statements to express your needs without shaming or blaming.
- Take the pressure off performance. Get rid of any scripts about how sex "should" look, and let yourselves be clumsy, awkward, and imperfect. Focus on pleasure and play rather than orgasms and positions.
- Explore new sexual activities together. Read sex advice books, listen to erotic podcasts, and try out different toys or kinks. The more you expand your sexual repertoire, the more connected and turned on you'll feel.

- Practice enthusiastic consent. Never pressure or guilt each other into sexual acts—only move forward when you're both "hell yes." Discuss your boundaries and safe words in advance.
- Get creative with non-sexual touch and affection. Explore different kinds of sensual contact, like massage, cuddling, bathing together, or eye-gazing. The more ways you experience physical intimacy, the deeper your sexual bond will be.

Remember, mind-blowing sex starts with a foundation of trust, respect, and emotional safety. Focus on cultivating those qualities in your overall relationship, and the sexual sparks will naturally follow. And don't be afraid to seek outside support from a sex therapist or workshop if you need guidance working through any erotic issues or inhibitions as a couple. Great sex is a skill like any other—it gets better with practice, communication, and expert advice!

Navigating Commitment, Monogamy, and Alternative Relationship Structures

One of the beautiful and befuddling things about being in a gay relationship today is how much freedom and flexibility we have to create the kind of partnerships we want. Unlike straight couples, we're not as bound by societal expectations of what our relationships should look like. Just a generation ago, most gay men couldn't even dream of living together openly, let alone getting married or building a family. So in a way, we're making up this whole 'gay commitment' thing as we go along.

At the same time, the lack of roadmaps and role models can make it tricky to navigate big questions like: What does commitment mean for us? Is lifelong monogamy realistic or even desirable? How do we cultivate security and stability while still honoring our sexual freedom and individuality? There's no one right way to answer these questions, but there are some key principles and conversations every gay couple should engage in as they chart their own course. Let's break it down:

Defining Commitment and Relationship Agreements

A critical conversation for any serious couple is defining what you mean by commitment and what kind of relationship structure you want to build together. For some, commitment means lifelong monogamy and all the traditional markers: living together, getting married, merging finances, raising a family, and growing old in matching rocking chairs. For others, it can look like living apart but still considering each other as primary partners, or being emotionally monogamous but sexually open, or committing to a time-bound container like a 5-year contract with the option to renew. The possibilities are endless.

There's no right or wrong way to commit, but it's essential that you're on the same page about your desires and expectations. Some key questions to discuss together are:

- What does commitment mean to each of us? What are we saying "yes" to, and what are we saying "no" to?
- What are our agreements around monogamy and exclusivity? Are we fully closed, open to certain kinds of sexual exploration, or somewhere in between?
- How will we handle attractions and flirtations outside our relationship? What's okay and what's not in terms of interacting with other guys?

- If we're open or poly, what are our boundaries and communication agreements around hooking up or dating others? How will we practice safer sex and protect each other's sexual health?
- What are our long-term visions for this relationship? Where do we see ourselves in 5, 10, or 20 years? Do our future desires line up?
- How will we continue to honor these agreements and check in about our evolving needs and boundaries over time?

Having these conversations early often creates a foundation of transparency, trust, and shared expectations that protects your relationship even as your desires and life circumstances evolve. And putting your commitments in writing, whether through a formal relationship contract or a signed page in your journal, helps make them tangible and accountable. You can always renegotiate as you go, but starting with a clear, mutual understanding prevents a world of pain and conflict down the line.

Monogamy and its Discontents

Let's be honest—long-term monogamy is hard for a lot of people, regardless of sexual orientation. The idea of choosing one partner for life and never being sexually or romantically involved with anyone else is a pretty tall order, especially for gay men. We're stereotypically (if not always accurately) cast as promiscuous, non-monogamous, and incapable of commitment. And it's true that hookup culture, open relationships, and alternative relationship structures are more common and accepted in the gay community.

But just because lifelong monogamy is challenging for many and not the only option doesn't mean it's not a viable path for gay men who seek it. Many same-sex couples are extremely fulfilled by the intimacy, security, and simplicity that monogamy provides, and report higher relationship satisfaction and longevity than their non-monogamous peers. It takes intentional communication, clear boundaries, and a whole lot of vulnerability and trust—but for those who desire it, it's well worth the effort.

If you and your partner are considering a monogamous commitment, here are some important points to keep in mind:

- Be radically honest about your sexual desires, history, and challenges with monogamy from the beginning. The more upfront you are, the less chance there is for painful surprises and betrayals down the line.
- Understand that monogamy is a practice, not a perfect state to achieve. You will both continue to feel attractions and urges for other people—what matters is how you communicate and handle those moments together.
- Don't use monogamy as a band-aid for deeper relationship issues like insecurity, mistrust, or unresolved trauma. Those issues will persist whether you're monogamous or not; get support to address them directly.
- Cultivate a rich and satisfying erotic life within your relationship. Try new sex positions and activities, share fantasies, and keep flirting like you're still trying to woo each other. Boredom and stagnancy are monogamy's greatest foes.

- If you do experience infidelity or a breach of your monogamy agreement, address it head-on with raw honesty and professional support. Rebuilding trust is possible if you're both willing to do the deep work of healing.

Remember, there's no shame in admitting that lifelong monogamy doesn't work for you, even if you truly love your partner. It's far better to craft a relationship agreement that fits your authentic needs than to keep failing at one that doesn't. The key is being rigorously honest with yourself and each other, and staying open to creative solutions.

Alternative Relationship Structures

Of course, monogamy is far from the only option for committed gay couples these days. Many are exploring alternative relationship structures that allow for some degree of sexual or romantic openness while still maintaining a strong primary bond. These can take many forms, such as:

- **Monogamish:** A mostly monogamous relationship that allows for occasional exceptions or specific kinds of outside sexual activity, like on vacation or with a pre-approved friend.
- **Sexually open relationship:** Partners are emotionally exclusive but free to pursue casual sex with others, often under certain agreed-upon circumstances or guidelines.
- **Polyamory:** Having multiple romantic and/or sexual partners at once, with the full knowledge and consent of everyone involved. This can take many forms, like a primary couple that each has additional partners or a non-hierarchical network of lovers.

- **Relationship anarchy:** Rejecting traditional relationship categories and hierarchies altogether, and letting each individual connection find its own level and form fluidly over time.

Navigating any kind of non-monogamy requires next-level communication, transparency, and trust between partners. It's not for the avoidant or faint of heart. Some key things to keep in mind:

- Create clear agreements and boundaries around your openness, and err on the side of over-communicating about your activities. Sneaking around and lying always makes things worse.
- Prioritize the primacy and well-being of your core relationship. Opening up won't fix existing issues and can often amplify them. Make sure you're rock solid as a couple before inviting others in.
- Practice impeccable sexual health and safety for everyone involved. Get regularly tested, use condoms and/or PrEP consistently, and have a plan for how to handle potential STI exposures or scares.
- Be prepared to feel all the feels. Jealousy, insecurity, fear, and a sense of loss are common companions to non-monogamy, especially in the beginning. Get support and resources to work through the tough emotions that come up.
- Respect that not every gay man, or even every horny gay man, wants to be your third or side piece. Only pursue guys who enthusiastically consent to being part of your arrangement.

Just like monogamy, open relationships, and polyamory are full-time jobs of communication and emotional labor. Never assume they'll be easier or more natural just because you're gay. But for those with self-awareness, relational skills, and a genuine desire for sexual novelty combined with romantic depth, alternative structures can be immensely fulfilling.

Ultimately, there's no one "gay way" to do commitment and relationships. What matters is that you and your partner are rigorously honest with yourselves and each other about your true needs and desires, and co-create an agreement that works for you both. That may change and evolve many times over the course of your life together, and that's okay. The hottest, juiciest, and most soul-satisfying gay love comes from continuously choosing each other consciously, whatever that looks like for you.

The key is to stay curious, communicative, and compassionate with each other as you navigate the ups and downs of gay commitment. Be willing to have tough conversations, to own your sh*t, to apologize and forgive, and to stretch and grow in service of your love. Remember that you're on the same team, fighting for the same future together. When in doubt, choose each other over and over again.

And if, at some point, you realize that you're no longer a match, have the courage to let each other go with love. Honor the journey you've shared and the lessons you've learned. Trust that ending a relationship that's no longer serving you both is not a failure but a profound act of love and respect.

What matters most is that you stay true to yourself and your evolving needs and desires as a gay man on this wild, unpredictable adventure of love and life. Don't get too caught up in labels, logistics, or trying to force a fit where there isn't one. Focus on building a relationship that feels honest, nourishing, and expansive to your soul, one day at a time. The rest will work itself out.

And know that whatever your relationship status or structure, you are whole and worthy of love, just as you are. A partner is the cherry on top of an already delicious sundae—not the dish itself. Keep cultivating a life of passion, purpose, and community outside of your romantic relationships, and let that be the foundation from which you love and commit to another. That's the secret to sustainable, satisfying gay love in all its many colors and configurations.

Chapter 5:

Sex and Intimacy

Developing a Healthy, Shame-Free Sexuality

Many of us grow up absorbing toxic messages that our sexual desires are sinful, disgusting, or abnormal, and we're taught to fear, suppress, or feel ashamed of our erotic truth. Undoing that early programming and embracing our sexuality as healthy, natural, and beautiful is a crucial part of thriving as gay men since being gay and having a loving and celebratory relationship with sexuality is our greatest gift.

Cultivating a truly joyful, empowered sexual self is a lifelong journey for the most part, as it requires consciously examining our beliefs and attitudes, releasing internalized homophobia, and practicing radical self-acceptance one day at a time.

For developing a healthy, shame-free sexuality, practice the following principles:

Recognize the Truth and Naturality in Your Desires

Same-sex desire is not an aberration, even though it might be a natural expression of human sexuality that has existed throughout history. No matter what messages you may have internalized from religion, family, or society, know that you are perfectly normal and lovable just as you are, and there is nothing wrong with being attracted to and aroused by other men.

Take some time to reflect on the specific negative beliefs you hold about your sexuality. Notice what comes up when you think about gay sex—is it excitement and pleasure, or fear and disgust? Do you have judgments about certain sex acts being "dirty" or "wrong"? Identifying these inner critics is the first step to diffusing their power.

When shame arises, practice meeting it with compassion and affirmation. Remind yourself that your desires are natural, innocent, and shared by millions of healthy, ethical people worldwide. Imagine yourself as a young child—tender, curious, and longing to love and be loved. Can you extend compassion to him, and are all the parts of you still carrying his shame? With time and intention, you can re-parent your inner sexual self and reclaim the joyful birthright of erotic innocence.

Educate Yourself About Gay Sexual Health and Pleasure

Many gay men enter adulthood with a lot of misconceptions and missing information about sex. You may have a lot of basic questions and anxieties about how to have sex, how to stay safe, and what's normal if you grew up without any positive models for gay intimacy or never received a queer-inclusive sex education.

One of the best antidotes to sexual ignorance and shame is accurate, sex-positive information. Make a commitment to educating yourself about your miraculous gay body and all the ways you can experience erotic bliss. Some great resources include:

LGBTQ-focused sex advice books like "The Joy of Gay Sex," "The Ultimate Guide to Anal Sex for Men," or "How to Top Like a

Porn Star." These provide clear, shameless guidance on everything from basic anatomy to advanced techniques (Amazon.com, 2024).

Secondly, you can find queer sex education websites like Scarleteen or Advocates for Youth, which offer comprehensive, affirming info on sexual health, pleasure, and communication for LGBTQ folks (Corinna, 2010).

The next way to discover ways to have safe sex is through workshops or classes on topics like anal sex, BDSM, tantra, or sexual communication. Many sex toy shops, LGBTQ centers, and kink organizations offer these regularly. Learning in a community can be a powerful way to normalize your desires and pick up new skills.

You can also learn tricks through pornography that depicts gay sex realistically and ethically. While mainstream porn often promotes unhealthy stereotypes, there are creators making beautiful, consensual erotic media for a gay audience. Look for studios like CockyBoys, Himeros.tv, or Indie Porn Revolution (Povey, 2023).

You will be equipped to experience it safely and ecstatically if you learn about the ins and outs of gay sex. Knowledge is empowerment, and by filling in the gaps in your erotic education, you can transform fear and uncertainty into savvy and skill.

Explore Your Body and Desires Through Solo Sex

Masturbation is one of the best ways to develop an authentic, joyful gay sexuality, independent of anyone else's judgments or expectations. Through patient solo exploration, you can discover your unique erogenous zones, fantasies, and orgasmic potential without any pressure to perform.

If you struggle with sexual shame, masturbation is an especially powerful practice for healing and reclamation. By lavishing your body with your own love and attention, you affirm that your pleasure is sacred and deserving of celebration. You literally become your own best lover.

You can make the experience of self-pleasure delightful by setting aside ample time in a private, comfortable place where you won't be disturbed. Create an ambiance that helps you feel safe and sensual—maybe candles, music, or luxurious towels. When the mood is all set, start with deep breathing and a gentle, loving touch all over your body. Caress your skin like you're precious. Arousal begins way before genital contact. You can experiment with different strokes, pressures, techniques, and fantasies. Be curious about what lights up your unique erotic wiring. Let yourself make noise and move in whatever ways feel good, without judgment. The next tip to enjoy the self-pleasure experience is to feel free to incorporate toys like dildos, vibrators, or masturbation sleeves. These can add delicious variety and intensity to your solo repertoire. As part of foreplay, you can enjoy erotic media that turns you on, whether that's porn, sexy stories, or your own imagination. There's no shame in any fantasy between consenting adults. Lastly, expand your definition of what "counts" as sex. Masturbation doesn't have to end in ejaculation to be pleasurable and valid. Enjoy the journey of arousal without fixating on the finish line.

The more you make masturbation a regular act of self-care, the more at home you'll feel in your erotic skin. Your solo sexuality is the foundation upon which you'll build healthy, authentic intimacy with others. By giving yourself generous, shameless pleasure, you fill your own cup and model how you want to be touched by a partner.

Practice Clear Sexual Communication With Partners

While self-love is key, shame-free sexuality truly blossoms in the communion of two (or more) people celebrating each other's erotic truths. Intimacy reaches its greatest depths when we feel safe enough to reveal our raw desires and have them lovingly received. That's why honest, courageous sexual communication with partners is so essential.

We expect our partners to read our minds and just know how to please us, as many of us struggle to talk openly about sex due to various reasons like shyness, shame, or fear of rejection. But no one is a mind-reader, and bottling up our needs only breeds resentment and disconnection. Learning to ask for what we want and navigate our differences is a cornerstone of great gay sex.

You can have productive conversations about sex with a partner by simply starting the conversation at a neutral time, not in the heat of the moment. Let your partner know you want to talk about your sex life and set aside intentional time to do so.

While you are discussing such a tender topic, try using "I" statements to express your desires, fantasies, and boundaries to avoid criticism or blame. Instead of saying, "I would love to try prostate massage together" vs. "You never touch my prostate."

Thirdly, you need to get specific about what feels good, what doesn't, and what you want more or less of. Vague feedback like "That was hot" is less helpful than "I love it when you kiss my neck."

Try approaching sex as a team effort, not a zero-sum game, by framing your requests as experiments to explore together, not demands. Be open to compromise and finding win-wins.

Just in case, if you have a hard time verbalizing in the moment, consider developing some simple hand signals or nonverbal cues to communicate. You might squeeze your partner's hand twice to mean "more pressure" or make a peace sign to mean "let's take a break."

Finally, always remember that you have the right to slow down, stop, or change your mind at any point during a sexual encounter, no matter what you initially agreed to. Practice saying "no" or "pause," and know your partner will respect it.

It will become easier and more natural if you flex your sexual communication muscles, as your partner will appreciate your honesty and direction. People generally want to be good lovers and just need a little guidance to get there.

Of course, it takes two to tango—all the communication skills in the world won't help if your partner consistently shuts down, shames you, or disregards your needs. Never tolerate coercion, mockery, or pressure when it comes to sex. If you come across such a thing, it's time to have a serious conversation about your sexual compatibility. You deserve a partner who celebrates your vulnerability and meets it with care.

Embrace Your Inner Erotic Creature

At the end of the day, developing a shame-free sexuality is about coming home to your own wild erotic nature. It's about embracing the fact that you are—we all are—sexual beings with a vast capacity for ecstasy, intimacy, and union. That's not a flaw or a joke; it's a divine gift and a sacred responsibility.

When we live in a sex-negative, homophobic culture, embracing our erotic truth is a radical act. It's a huge "f*ck you" to a system that profits from our shame and disconnection. Every time we choose authentic sexual expression over social censure; we create a more liberated world for ourselves and each other.

So start befriending your inner erotic creature, in whatever form it takes. Get to know your unique turn-ons and wet dreams. Court your kinks and edge-play with compassion. Unleash your inner slut, siren, or sexual shaman, as you will experience more bliss and vibrancy in all areas of life if you live up to the wild and untamable parts of your sexuality.

And remember, there's no finish line when it comes to shame-free sexuality. Unlearning a lifetime of sex-negativity and homophobia is a process, not a destination. You'll probably always have moments of doubt, insecurity, and inner conflict around sex. The key is to meet them with even more love and healthy outlets for connection.

Keep filling your mind with positive, celebratory messages about queer sexuality. Surround yourself with people and experiences that reflect your joy and hotness back to you. And most of all, keep showing up for your own erotic growth, day after day, with all the compassion and care you deserved from the start. Because your sweet gay body is precious, and your pleasure matters. Period.

Common Sexual Interests and Practices Among Gay Men

Gay male sexuality is a rich, diverse tapestry of desires, behaviors, and relationship styles. From vanilla to kinky, monogamous to multi-partnered, tops to bottoms, and beyond, there's an endless array of ways that queer men express and experience erotic love. While no two gay men are exactly alike in bed (or in life), there are some common sexual interests and practices that shape the cultural landscape of gay intimacy.

Versatility of Anal Sex

It is true that for many gay guys, there's nothing quite like the physical closeness and prostate pleasure of penetrative sex, and it is considered the defining sex act for gay men. But the truth is, not all gay men love anal sex or do it all the time. According to a report, less than 40% of gay men have anal sex on a regular basis, as many prefer other activities like oral sex, mutual masturbation, frottage (rubbing against each other), or just plain passionate kissing. And some gay men never have anal sex at all, because of preference, pain, or past trauma—and that's totally okay! An aversion to anal doesn't make you any less gay or sexually fulfilled.

For the gay men who do enjoy anal play, there's a common concept of "top," "bottom," and "versatile" roles. A top is typically the insertive partner (the one doing the penetrating), a bottom is receptive (the one being penetrated), and someone who enjoys both is considered versatile. Some guys have a strong preference for one role or the other, while others like to switch it up based on mood and partner.

While top and bottom labels are useful shorthands, it's important not to get too caught up in rigid sexual roles or make assumptions about someone based on theirs. Bottoms can be masculine and dominant, tops can be shy and submissive, and your anal role is not indicative of your personality or worth. All combinations are valid and valuable.

For gay couples who plan to explore anal sex, they need to consider a few tips for doing it safely and pleasurably.

The first and foremost tip is to start slow and use lots of lube, as unlike the vagina, the anus does not self-lubricate, and having some good-quality silicone or water-based lube on hand is a must for comfortable penetration.

Secondly, prep with plenty of foreplay, rimming, fingering, or toy play before attempting penetration, as this helps relax the sphincter muscles and makes the experience much more enjoyable for both partners.

Don’t forget to use condoms and get tested regularly for STIs, including HIV. Anal sex carries a higher risk of transmission than other activities, so safer sex practices are key. Consider going on PrEP (pre-exposure prophylaxis) if you're not in a sexually exclusive relationship (Newcomb et al., 2018).

Also, try to communicate openly with your partner about your desires, boundaries, and comfort levels. Don't be shy to give feedback and ask for what you need in the moment, whether that's a change of position or more lube.

Finally, if you experience pain or bleeding during anal sex, stop and consult a gay-friendly doctor. Apparently some discomfort is normal, but acute pain is a sign that something is wrong, so don't just grin and bear it—your butt deserves TLC!

Oral Sex and Rimming

Oral sex is a beloved staple in the gay erotic diet. Sucking and licking each other's cocks, balls, and butts is a delicious way to give and receive pleasure with relatively low risk. For many gay men, oral is their preferred main course and can be just as intimate and satisfying as anal.

Blowjobs are an especially popular pastime for their versatility and accessibility. They can be a hot appetizer before other play, a tasty treat all on their own, or a soothing nightcap after more intense activities. And unlike anal sex, oral is easy to do almost anywhere—in the car, at the club, under your desk at work (just kidding... unless?). All you need is a willing mouth and some tasty meat.

Some tips for mind-blowing BJs include that you communicate with your partner about what feels good. Everyone likes different types of pressure, speed, suction, etc. Asking for feedback and direction is the key to being a star cocksucker.

Try using your hands as well as your mouth. Stroke the shaft while sucking the head, cup and caress the balls, and play with the perineum and prostate. Mixing up sensations keeps it spicy. Moreover, watch the teeth! While some guys enjoy a little nibble, accidental chomps are never fun. Keep your lips curled over your teeth if you're going deep or bobbing fast.

The final question is: To swallow or not to swallow? It is purely a personal choice with no right answer. If you choose to let him come into your mouth, position the head on or past your tongue to avoid gagging, but if you'd rather not, let your partner know in advance so he can pull out in time.

Another popular oral activity among gay men is rimming, or analingus—using your tongue and mouth to stimulate your partner's anus. Because the anus is full of sensitive nerve endings, this can be an incredibly pleasurable and intimate act.

However, rimming does carry some risks. The anus contains bacteria that can lead to hepatitis, parasites, or other infections if ingested. To rim more safely, it is suggested to use a dental dam, a cut-open condom, or plastic wrap as a barrier between your mouth and his anus. Also, try to make sure that you both wash thoroughly with soap and water before getting started. Thirdly, it is highly important to avoid rimming if either of you have cuts or sores in your mouth or anal region. Finally, consider getting vaccinated for hepatitis A and B, which can be contracted through rimming.

With a little preparation and communication, rimming can be a wonderfully erotic addition to your oral repertoire. Many gay men find it to be an especially bonding and electrifying experience. Bon Appetit!

Fetish Play, Kink, and BDSM

The gay male community has a long, storied relationship with kink and BDSM (bondage and discipline, dominance and submission, sadism and masochism). From the hanky code of the 70s to the ubiquity of leather gear, queer men have often been at the vanguard of sexual experimentation and adventurousness.

You certainly don't have to be into kink to have a satisfying sex life, but for many, exploring power dynamics, sensation play, role-playing, and other "non-vanilla" erotic practices is a huge turn-on and source of fulfillment. Some common kinks among gay men include:

Dom/Sub Play

Consensually enacting a power dynamic in which one partner (the Dom) takes psychological and/or physical control over the other (the sub) within negotiated boundaries. This can involve anything from light spanking and ordering around to more intense scenes with restraints, punishment, or service.

Bondage

Using ropes, cuffs, tape, or other materials to restrict a partner's movement for erotic and/or aesthetic purposes. Being bound can heighten physical sensations and surrender while tying someone up can evoke feelings of power and possession.

Impact Play

Purposefully giving or receiving pain with tools like floggers, paddles, whips, or hands. The endorphin rush and cathartic release of intense sensation can be deeply erotic and emotionally bonding for many people. It requires a lot of trust, communication, and anatomical knowledge to do it safely.

Some other common kinks in the gay male world include:

Role-play and Fantasy

Acting out sexy scenarios like doctor/patient, teacher/student, cop/criminal, etc., or embodying archetypal roles like "the innocent virgin" or "the insatiable slut." Costumes, dirty talk, and props can all enhance the sense of psychological immersion.

Feet and Shoes

Foot worship, toe sucking, trampling, "forced" foot smelling, shoe licking, etc. For many gay men, feet are a highly charged erotic zone and a symbol of masculine power, vulnerability, and/or humiliation.

Watersports

Erotic play involving urine, whether that's peeing on or in someone, "making" them drink piss, clothes wetting, or holding it in for agonizing arousal. The warm wetness, dominance, humiliation, and sheer taboo are all part of the thrill.

Group Sex

MMF threesomes, gang bangs, fuck trains, sex parties—many gay men are turned on by the idea of taking on multiple men at once or watching their partner do so. The visual feast, the anything-goes vibe, and the sense of being used can be super hot.

Anonymous Sex

Gloryhole BJs, cruising, bathhouse hookups—the danger and unknown of getting it on with a total stranger taps into deep, primal urges. The lack of strings or emotional intimacy can be freeing for some and empty for others.

Whatever your kinks or curiosities, the key to exploring them in a healthy way is consent, communication, trust, and information. Educate yourself on the techniques, tools, and safety precautions for your desired activity before diving in. Negotiate clear boundaries and safe words with your partner(s). Start slow and check in often. And make sure you have sexy aftercare rituals in place to help everyone feel grounded and cared for post-play.

Remember, your kinks and fantasies are a healthy, natural part of your erotic wiring, not a shameful perversion. You get to write your own gay sex script, page by page. Don't let anyone police your sexual imagination or desires—as long as everyone involved is a consenting adult, you're free to get as freaky as you want to be. Life's too short for boring, beige sex. So strap on, lube up, and let your gay kink flag fly.

Importance of Consent, Communication, and Safety

While gay sex can be fun, freeing, and fabulously pleasurable, it also comes with real physical and emotional risks. From STIs to consent violations to boundary breaches, sex has the potential to harm as well as heal. That's why conscious communication, impeccable safety practices, and an unwavering commitment to mutual care are just as important as sexual technique.

At the beating heart of great gay sex—really, any sex—is consent. More than just the absence of "no," consent is the enthusiastic, ongoing "yes!" to engage in erotic contact of any kind. It's the foundation of trust that allows us to let our guards down and surrender to ecstasy together.

Here are some key principles of sexual consent:

- Consent must be freely given, without pressure, coercion, or intoxication. If someone seems hesitant or ambivalent, that's not consent. Only a clear, excited "yes" counts.

- Consent must be specific. Agreeing to one sex act (like oral) doesn't imply consent to others (like anal). It's important to check in throughout an encounter and not make assumptions.
- Consent is reversible. Even if the consenting partner has already started fooling around, that doesn't mean he has lost the right to stop in the middle. He has the right to change his mind, set a boundary, and revoke consent at any point without giving any explanation.
- Consent should be informed. That means disclosing any STIs, relationship agreements, or other factors that may affect someone's decision to be intimate with you, as lying or withholding key info undermines consent.
- Consent isn't a one-time event. Just because someone consented to sex before doesn't mean you have a standing invitation. Consent must be established freshly in each encounter and moment.
- In practice, consensual gay sex looks like a whole lot of communication! Contrary to what porn or locker room talk would have you believe, great lovers are collaborators, not mind-readers. They ask for what they want plainly, listen deeply, and course-correct often.

Here are some examples of sexy consent communication in action:

- "I've been wanting to taste your cock all night. Can I suck you?"
- "Does this feel good? Do you want it harder or slower?"

- "I'm really turned on, but I don't feel ready for anal tonight. Can we stick to oral and hands for now?"
- "I'd love to rim you, but my last STI test was a few months ago. Are you cool with using a dental dam?"
- "Hey, let's take a quick snack break and cuddle, feeling a little overstimulated."
- "That was so hot. Next time, can we try that position with me on top?"

Talking during sex may feel clumsy at first, but most guys find it incredibly bonding and arousing. By asking for desires directly and responding to feedback in real-time, you create a feedback loop that deepens turn-on and trust. You learn exactly how your partner likes to be touched, and you get to experience the electric thrill of being craved out loud.

Of course, consent is far from the only crucial conversation to have around gay sex. Negotiating safer sex practices, STI and HIV status, and relationship agreements are also key pieces of the hot sex puzzle.

Before you jump into bed with someone new (or as soon as possible after a spontaneous hookup), make sure to have a clear discussion about the last time you were each tested for STIs and HIV, and the results. Also, discuss your safer sex practices (condoms, PrEP, TasP, etc.). Do let him know if you may have any STIs currently and how you're treating them. It is equally important to discuss your relationship status and relevant agreements (monogamous, open, etc.), your sexual desires, boundaries, and expectations for this encounter (Mitchell et al., 2016).

Having these convos can feel unsexy in the moment, but they're so worth it for the peace of mind and respect they bring. By being upfront about your status and safety needs, you show your partner that your health and well-being are the ultimate aphrodisiac.

Beyond negotiating consent and sexual logistics, learning to communicate your erotic fantasies, vulnerable desires, and secret turn-ons is a powerful bonding practice. Sharing the tender truths of your sexuality creates a container of raw intimacy where magic can happen.

Of course, pillow talk is a delicate dance, as it helps you tread carefully with a new partner. Many of us have wounds and insecurities about our sexual worthiness. It is better to start by sharing milder fantasies or memories and see how they respond. If they react with openness and enthusiasm, you can slowly peel back the layers to your spicier core erotic self.

Some General Guidelines for Sexy Sharings

First of all, frame sensitive desires as "the thought of [X] really turns me on," not "I want you to do [X] to me." Let your partner respond with their level of interest before applying direct pressure.

Secondly, if your partner shares a fantasy you're not into, thank them for their vulnerability and suggest an alternative you're both excited about. For example, "Mmm, role-playing a professor/student scene isn't really my thing, but I'd love to explore that naughty vibe with some light spanking instead."

Thirdly, if you have a kinky request, present it with reassurance and an easy out. Something like: "I've always wanted to try getting tied up, but there's no pressure at all if that's not your bag. I'm also really turned on by the idea of you holding my hands down while you ride me, if you prefer that."

Eventually, when hearing a partner's deep desires, respond with curiosity and compassion, even if it's not your thing. Thank them for trusting you, and be gentle with any tender spots. Never shame or judge someone for their turn-ons.

As you grow more secure in your erotic communication skills, you may find yourself craving next-level sexual adventures like threesomes, kink scenes, or sex parties. These can be incredibly hot and fun, but they also require extra layers of negotiation and safety planning.

Before you attend a play party or invite that cute couple home from the bar, be sure to get clear on your boundaries and agreements with your partner(s) in advance. What sex acts, positions, or dynamics are on and off the table? Will you be fluidly bonded only with each other? Who can do what with whom?

Also, determine a safe word that means "stop everything immediately." The stoplight system of "green = keep going, yellow = ease up, red = stop right now" works well for many. Moreover, make them agree on a discrete check-in signal in case things feel off in the heat of the moment. Knowing you can subtly squeeze your partner's hand or catch their eye to pause the action creates a lot of security.

Also, never forget to pack safer sex supplies like condoms, lube, gloves, dental dams, toys, and anything else you'll need to protect everyone's bodies and boundaries.

Be mindful to give yourself blanket permission to slow down, change your mind, or leave at any time; no explanation is needed.

Pushing yourself to keep going when you're checked out or upset is a recipe for trauma and resentment.

Lastly, after the big event, plan for some tender aftercare. Make space to debrief with your partner(s), share vulnerabilities, and reaffirm your bond. Group sex and kink can bring up all kinds of intense emotions, so be extra loving with yourself and each other.

The key to expanding your sexual horizons safely and ethically is to go at the pace of the slowest partner, check in often, and err on the side of over-communicating. By building trust and care into your freaky fun, you create a secure container to let your wildest fantasies run free, and that's when things get really magic.

At the end of the day, consent, communication, and safety are the holy trinity of phenomenal sex and relationships. You honor your own precious erotic self and ensure your partners feel cherished and secure by making them the non-negotiable foundation of your love life. You create a sexual culture of mutual reverence and delight, and there's nothing hotter than that.

Emotional Intimacy and Vulnerability

For most gay men, the ultimate sexual high isn't just a mind-blowing orgasm (although the goddess knows that's fabulous); it's the profound feeling of being seen, accepted, and even adored in your rawest, realest self. It's that delicious melting of individual boundaries into a pulsing circuit of shared ecstasy and energetic union leading to deep intimacy.

When you strip away all the techniques, toys, and tricks, intimate sex is about receiving and offering exquisite mutual vulnerability. It's about exposing your tender underbelly and having it licked and loved on. It's about pressing even your scariest, shadowiest bits right up against another's and whispering, "I want you, all of you," into the dark.

For many queer men, the hardest part of sex is accessing that level of trust and self-disclosure. It means moving past performative games and good-boy masks into the vulnerable heart of our authentic desire, which requires relinquishing the defenses that have kept us safe and separate for so long and daring to put our real needs on the table.

Intimacy also requires presence—showing up fully in each moment without distraction or disassociation. When you're intimate with someone, you're not performing the part of a hot stud or a power bottom, nor are you lost in a fantasy of someone else or watching yourself from above. You're right here, breathing, beating, and baring it all in real time.

So the real question would be, how do we open up to deeper sexual intimacy? Like any muscle, vulnerability takes practice and intention to grow. You can cultivate more emotional nakedness in your sex life in the following ways:

Share Your Inner Emotional World

During sex, we tend to focus on sensations and visuals—how things look and feel in our bodies. But there's a whole rich inner world of memories, self-talk, emotional flavors, and subtle energetic shifts that often go unexpressed. It feels empowering to let your partner into that vulnerable space.

The next time you're fooling around, try narrating your inner experience out loud. Not just the sexy clinical details but what's moving through you psychologically and emotionally. For example, "Mmm, I feel so safe and held when you touch me like that. It reminds me of being hugged as a kid and feeling totally at peace." Or you can utter, "Ah, I just had a little wave of nervousness come up. I think it's my old fear of letting go and being really seen during sex. But I want you to see all of me, even the scared bits." Or "I keep having this delicious full-body shiver every time you kiss my neck. It's like liquid honey spreading from that spot all the way down into my toes." Or "I'm feeling this yummy mix of tender and fierce energy right now. I want to be so gentle and reverent with you but also just devour you whole."

Receiving and responding to a partner's emotional share is just as vulnerable as offering your own. When your guy exposes his softer side, meet him with affirmation, appreciation, and lots of eye contact. Let him feel your loving presence, drinking in every word, and also reflect back on what you're hearing to show you get it.

You can also use physical touch to affirm your emotional attunement. If he shares a vulnerable fear, place a hand on his heart or cheek. If he's feeling sassy and flirty, squeeze his ass or nip at his ear, as responding to each other's inner worlds through all love languages creates an exquisite feedback loop of deepening trust and surrender.

Ask for Scary-Vulnerable Things

We all have secret erotic wishes that feel almost too tender to name. Maybe it's a deep longing to feel adored and worshipped by a partner. Maybe it's a desire to totally relinquish control and let someone else drive the sexual encounter, or maybe it's a craving to play with taboo power dynamics or be pushed outside your comfort zone.

The juicy intimacy magic happens when we risk revealing those private fantasies and letting a trusted partner play them out with us. By articulating our realest, rawest needs, we allow ourselves to be truly seen and met in our erotic truth, and that's when sex moves from performance to profound communion.

Of course, asking for our most vulnerable desires is scary as hell. What if our partner thinks we're too freaky or needy? What if they reject us or, worse, agree to play along inauthentically? Also, you might wonder if it's safer to just keep our erotic underbelly hidden and settled for "good enough" sex?

Yes, asking for what you want comes with emotional risk. Your partner may not be able to meet you there, and that can sting like hell, but by laying your truth on the line, you open up the possibility for incredible healing and affirmation, too, because there's no feeling quite like having your core erotic self received with reverence and delight.

Here are some examples of intimate erotic requests you can try with a trusted partner:

- "I have this deep yearning to feel really precious and adored during sex. Could you go super slow and worship every inch of my body with your lips and tell me how beautiful I am?"
- "I keep fantasizing about being totally ravished and not having to make any decisions. Would you be up for pinning me down and having your way with me, checking in as we go? I'll use the stoplight safe words if anything feels off."

- "There's this edgy dom/sub scene I've always wanted to try, but I've been scared to ask for it. It would look like you call me a "good boy" while you make me beg for your cock and fuck my throat. Is that something you'd be open to exploring with me?"

As always, frame your requests with reassurance and an easy out. Remind your partner that you adore them no matter what and that your fantasies aren't expectations or demands. Make it clear that you can mutually explore the hottest, safest version of your desire together or find another sexy adventure you both love. The goal is emotional intimacy through co-creation, not pressure or coercion.

Welcome All Emotions (not just the sexy ones)

Intense sexual intimacy stirs our deepest emotional soup. Sometimes, in moments of real energetic merging with a partner, grief, anger, or existential loneliness bubble up alongside the turn-on and craving, tears mix with sweat, and primal sobs erupt between ecstatic moans.

For many people, feeling big 'unsexy' emotions during sex is mortifying, and we scramble to choke them down and get back to the script of how we think sex should go. We worry our partner will be turned off or weirded out by our sudden vulnerability, so we hold our breath and double down on performing pleasure, even as our tender guts are spilling everywhere. But repressing our authentic emotional experience only robs sex of its true power: To unite us in our raw human realness. When we show our real inner worlds and have them held lovingly by a partner, something deep and lasting shifts inside us. We start to rewrite the story that says we're too much as we are.

Next time you feel a big scary-vulnerable feeling come up during sex (and you feel basically safe), try letting it move through you. Breathe into the sensation and physical expression that want to happen: tears, laughter, shudders, deep sighs, grunts, or growls. Make space for all the beautiful, messy humans you are.

If your partner seems confused or startled by your emotional release, reassure them that you're okay and that releasing emotions is welcome and healing for you. Invite them to breathe and be with you in that tender space without trying to fix anything. Let them bear witness to your humanity, and thank them sincerely for the gift of their presence.

Of course, if an emotion feels too overwhelming or triggered, it's absolutely fine to slow down, ask for a break, or stop sex altogether. Part of emotional intimacy is honoring your own authenticity and bandwidth in each moment. Never pressure yourself to perform vulnerability when you're actually in distress and need support. Your partner should cheer on your self-honesty and self-advocacy, not criticize you for breaking an erotic script.

Communicate Vulnerably Outside of Sex, too

Intimacy in the bedroom depends on the quality of your emotional bond in daily life, as true intimacy requires a foundation of trust and care across contexts. If you and your partner lack tools for navigating scary conversations, giving and receiving feedback, and expressing your real needs and feelings, that disconnect will inevitably bleed into your sex life.

Some ways to build that foundation include sharing your sexual history openly, including past traumas, insecurities, or shame you're still healing, and getting your partner all the way into your erotic inner world.

Secondly, offer loving reflections on your partner's strengths and growth areas as a lover, praise their unique sexual superpowers, and request more of the specific things that light you up. Moreover, when you feel triggered or reactive during a sexual encounter, call a timeout and express your tender emotions nonviolently. Remember that conflict is just growth trying to happen, and any ruptures can be repaired with good-faith communication.

Thirdly, after intense sexual experiences, make space to debrief and share aftercare. Check in about your favorite moments, what felt edgy, and what could make next time even better to affirm your love and care beyond the erotic charge.

Lastly, make a regular practice of naming appreciations and sweet memories from your sexual highlight reel to let your partner feel cherished and reflected outside the heat of the moment.

By tending to your relational ecosystem consciously and consistently, you create the optimal conditions for your next-level sexual intimacy to bloom. You can relax into each erotic encounter, knowing you've built a crash pad of mutual acceptance to fall back on.

At the end of the day, emotional intimacy during sex isn't about performing vulnerability or forcing a deep connection. It's about showing up authentically in each moment, witnessing and cherishing each other's humanity, and allowing the full spectrum of your emotional truth to be welcomed. It's about creating an erotic container strong and safe enough to hold you both at your most tender, exposed, and real. In that space of courageous mutual vulnerability, the potential for pleasure, healing, and transformation is truly boundless.

Chapter 6:

Dealing With Homophobia and Discrimination

The painful reality of homophobia and discrimination haunts us, ranging from microaggressions of everyday interactions and overt hate crimes to anti-gay bias, as an undeniable part of the queer experience in many areas of life. In order to cater to the situation, learning to cope with homophobia is an essential survival skill.

Before delving into strategies to cope with homophobia, it's pertinent to know what it really is? And how does it reflect in our lives? At its core, homophobia is the irrational fear, hatred, disgust, or prejudice against gay people; in simpler words, it tends to prove that same-sex attraction is unnatural and inferior. And it manifests itself not only in the behaviors of individuals but also in the fabric of our laws, institutions, and cultural norms.

The common examples of homophobia include:

- Using slurs like "f*g" or "homo" or making jokes that demean gay people.
- Assuming all gay men are feminine, promiscuous, or predatory.
- Excluding or ostracizing someone because of their sexual orientation.

- Denying services, housing, or employment to gay people.
- Opposing legal protections and rights for LGBTQ individuals.
- Perpetrating violence or hate crimes against gay men.
- Promoting the idea that homosexuality is a choice or a "lifestyle."
- Advocating for conversion therapy to "cure" same-sex attraction.

It is quite surprising to know that homophobia emanates not only from strangers but also from close family, coworkers, religious communities, and friends. Sometimes, it's blatant and unapologetic; other times, it's cloaked in concern or condescension. But no matter what form it takes, the impact of homophobia is always harmful.

Constant exposure to anti-gay talk makes us question our value and lovability and pushes us back into the closet in certain areas of life, leading to chronic stress, anxiety, depression, and even suicide. It keeps us looking over our shoulders, bracing for the next attack or rejection, and thus taking a serious toll on our mental health.

So how do we deal with the reality of homophobia without letting it crush our spirits? Here are some strategies for understanding and responding to anti-gay bias in empowered ways:

Recognize That Homophobia Is Not About You

When someone directs a homophobic comment or action your way, it's natural to feel attacked and take it personally, but it's crucial that you don't take it as a personal attack but rather as their bias, which has more to do with their own fears, ignorance, and unexamined prejudices, and you are not responsible for their hateful attitudes or behavior.

Homophobes lash out at gay people because our existence challenges their rigid ideas about gender, sexuality, and power just to cling to their set of beliefs. Their anti-gay venom is a reflection of their own insecurities and limitations, not your worth as a person. Visualize their words and energy passing right through you, like a gust of wind, and anchor yourself in the truth of your inherent goodness and dignity as a gay man, mentally repeating to yourself, "This isn't about you."

This doesn't mean the homophobic incident won't hurt you or make you angry; those feelings are valid and demand to be felt. But by not taking it personally, you rob the perpetrator of some of their perceived power over you and, on the contrary, preserve your sense of self.

Choose Your Battles

As much as we may want to, we can't single-handedly dismantle homophobia everywhere we encounter it. Trying to educate or call out every bigot who crosses our path would be exhausting and likely futile; instead, we should be selective and confront the only ones who are worth it.

Keep in mind the following questions to help you decide if it's worth engaging with a homophobe:

- Is this someone I have to interact with regularly (like a coworker or family member), or just a random stranger I'll never see again?

- Is there a power imbalance that would make speaking up risky for me (like with a boss or authority figure)?
- Is this person likely to be receptive to feedback, or are they deeply entrenched in their views?
- Am I in the right headspace to have this conversation calmly and effectively right now?
- Is there a chance of physical violence or retaliation if I confront them?
- Would saying something actually make me feel better and more empowered, or just drained?

There's no right or wrong answer—it's about trusting your judgment, honoring your energy levels in each situation, and knowing that a no-response can be empowering too. Silence can send a strong message that someone's words or actions are so beneath you that they don't even merit acknowledgment.

Other times, speaking up against homophobia is critical for setting boundaries and affirming your dignity. If someone is directly harassing, belittling you, or spouting hate in a shared space, letting it slide can eat away at your self-respect. In those moments, saying a firm "That's not okay" or "I won't tolerate being spoken to like that" can be tremendously empowering, even if they don't change their tune.

The key is to get clear on your non-negotiables and deal-breakers when it comes to homophobic treatment. Know ahead of time what you absolutely won't put up with, and have some go-to phrases for shutting it down swiftly. With everybody else, conserve your precious time and energy for more rewarding pursuits.

Lean on Your Support System

Experiencing homophobia can be incredibly isolating and demoralizing, which can make you feel bereft and cornered against the whole world despite having a solid support system. That's why it's so important to have a solid support system of people who love and affirm you unconditionally.

It is quite helpful to share with your queer friends about what happened when you had a run-in with homophobia and how it made you feel, to let them validate your pain and anger, and to remind them how fabulous and worthy you are. Vent, cry, laugh, rage—do whatever you need to release the toxic residue of the experience.

You can seek out queer community spaces where you can feel seen and supported by joining a gay sports league, volunteering with an LGBTQ organization, or finding an online forum for connecting with other gay men. Surround yourself with positive representation, and stories of queer resilience.

You can also look for support from straight allies who are committed to unlearning their own biases and fighting for equality. These may be coworkers, neighbors, or even family members who consistently show up for you and speak out against homophobia in their own circles. Let them know how much their allyship means to you, and lean on them when you need a listening ear or helping hand.

There is an entire community of people who have your back and want to share the burden of homophobia just to see you thrive as a gay man. Reach out early and often, and let their love buoy you through the tough times.

Practice Unapologetic Self-Love

The cruel part is when the constant bombardment of hate messages clips away our sense of pride, making us believe them on some level. We may find ourselves shrinking, apologizing for our existence, or trying to prove our value by being "good gays." That's why self-love and acceptance are the only panaceas for homophobia. The more we fill ourselves up with genuine appreciation for our gay selves, the less room there is for anyone else's negative opinions to take root. We develop a kind of psychological Teflon coating that lets homophobic glances and remarks slide right off.

Some ways to cultivate gay self-love:

First and foremost, surround yourself with positive queer representation in media, art, and culture. Seek out books, movies, music, and role models that reflect the joy and beauty of LGBTQ lives.

Second, practice self-affirmations that celebrate your sexuality by looking in the mirror each morning and declaring things like, "I am proud to be a gay man whose love is sacred and deserving of value and respect." Record yourself reciting them and listen often.

Third, treat yourself to gay-centered experiences and pleasures. Take a queer history walking tour, splurge on a rainbow accessory, and get a massage from a cute gay masseur. Infuse your daily life with gestures of gay delight and pride.

Fourth, volunteer or donate to LGBTQ causes you care about, as standing up for your community reinforces your own sense of dignity and agency as a gay person. Find ways to be of service that align with your skills and passions.

Last but not least, cultivate a fulfilling life outside of your sexual orientation by nourishing hobbies, friendships, and goals that celebrate your unique, awesome self. The more grounded you are in your own inherent worthiness, the less homophobes can shake you.

Self-love is a revolutionary act for any member of a marginalized group. By treating yourself with unshakable compassion, respect, and celebration, you send an energetic middle finger to anyone who would make you feel "less than." You become your own shelter from the storms of ignorance and hatred.

Turn Pain Into Purpose

Our personal experiences with homophobia can be an incredible fuel for creating positive change in the world. By channeling our righteous anger and heartache into activism, art, and community-building, we alchemize that pain into purpose by using the very thing meant to diminish us as a catalyst for transformation.

Look at all the queer trailblazers throughout history who refused to be silenced or shamed by a homophobic society. From Oscar Wilde to Audre Lorde to Harvey Milk, they took the injustice and injury of anti-gay oppression and fashioned it into fierce expressions of truth, beauty, and resistance. They turned slurs into battle cries and hate into a healer's power.

You can transmute your own brushes with homophobia into fuel for your passions and purpose by:

- Joining a gay rights organization and lobbying for protection and visibility.

- Creating art, music, or writing that expresses your queer perspective.
- Mentoring LGBTQ youth to help them navigate a homophobic world.
- Organizing queer social events and safe spaces in your community.
- Educating your straight friends and family about allyship and solidarity.
- Running for political office as an out-of-gay candidate.
- Living your life with joy, integrity, and pride as a big 'eff you' to haters.

We become part of a lineage of queer ancestors and activists who have been turning heartbreak into heroism for generations. We find meaning and fulfillment in the struggle, even on the hardest days, by using our collective pain as a catalyst for change.

The destruction of homophobia can be minimized by using it as fodder for liberation. By seeking to understand its roots, responding strategically, leaning on each other for support, and transmuting pain into purpose, we not only survive homophobia—we turn it on its head no matter how inescapable reality homophobia is. In the face of hate, choose love—for yourself, for your community, and for the better world you're co-creating with every courageous breath. That's the ultimate Gay Agenda.

Handling Workplace Discrimination

For many gay men, the workplace is one of the most stressful arenas for navigating homophobia and discrimination. Despite major strides in corporate LGBTQ inclusion over the past few decades, anti-gay bias still runs rampant in many professional settings. From casual homophobic jokes to denied promotions and outright harassment, workplace discrimination takes a heavy toll on our livelihoods and well-being.

The William Institute indicates that almost half of LGBTQ employees are fired, harassed, treated unfairly, and even passed over for jobs only because of their gender identity. Nearly 1 in 10 have left a job due to an unwelcoming environment. For many gay men, being out on the job is a calculated risk with real consequences.

We can protect ourselves and thrive as gay professionals in a still-homophobic corporate culture with wisdom and self-respect by adopting the following strategies:

Know Your Rights

First of all, you need to keep yourself abreast of legal laws pertaining to LGBTQ employees to combat workplace homophobia. Although we still have no such law protecting the rights of the mentioned minority class, the landmark decision of the Supreme Court in 2020 in Botstock v. Clayton County made anti-LGBTQ bias unlawful sex discrimination under Title VII of the Civil Rights Act (Liptak, 2020).

You have the right to file a complaint with the Equal Employment Opportunity Commission (EEOC) if you experience anti-gay discrimination on the job, including being fired, not hired, or otherwise mistreated in a company with 15 or more employees.

It is recommended to research what specific rights and remedies you have in your area, as plenty of states have laws to prohibit employee discrimination due to sexual orientation.

Knowing the lay of the legal land can give you a sense of security and empowerment when dealing with workplace homophobia. Even if you never end up taking formal action, just understanding what your employer can and can't get away with under the law is a kind of psychological armor. It reminds you that you're not just a helpless target but a gay man with rights and dignity.

Record All the Details

It is highly recommended that the details of every discrimination incident at work be documented. While you are at it, record the following details, particularly:

- What was said or done, and by whom.
- When and where it occurred.
- Any witnesses who saw or heard it.
- How it made you feel and impacted your work.
- What actions you took in response (if any).

It is understandable that you feel traumatic as the incident happens, but it is pertinent to write down the details while it's fresh in your mind. Save any relevant emails, texts, screenshots, or voicemails that support your account. Create a designated folder or notebook to keep track of everything in one place.

Having a clear, contemporaneous record of the discrimination you've faced serves several important purposes. First, it helps you process and validate your own experience. When homophobia happens, it's easy to second-guess or minimize what occurred, especially if it was subtle or if gaslighting is involved. Writing it down makes it concrete and harder to brush off.

Documentation also provides crucial evidence if you decide to report discrimination to HR or file a legal complaint. Your case will be stronger if you have more specific details and supporting materials. Even if you never end up using it formally, just knowing you have receipts can give you a sense of control and leverage in a difficult situation.

Finally, keeping track of homophobic incidents can reveal patterns over time that you may not notice in the moment. If you see that the same coworker keeps making snide comments or that you're repeatedly passed over for opportunities, that's valuable data for deciding how to respond and protect yourself moving forward.

Cultivate Backing and Build Allies

It's easy to feel like you're in it alone or that speaking up will just paint a target on your back, especially if you are the only gay person in your company or team. Seeking out allies and support systems both inside and outside of work will make you feel less isolated.

Start by identifying any coworkers or managers who seem LGBTQ-friendly and have your back. These may be other queer folks or straight allies who consistently speak up against homophobia and support diversity and inclusion. You can build allies around them by reaching out to them one-on-one and sharing what you've been experiencing. Once you are sure they are with you, you can ask them for their moral support or even as an eyewitness to help you fight the case for discrimination.

If your company has an LGBTQ employee resource group (ERG), join it and get involved. These affinity groups can provide a safe space for connecting with other queer colleagues, sharing resources, and strategizing for change. They often have the ear of senior leadership and can help raise awareness of discrimination issues.

You can also look for support outside of your immediate workplace. Seek out professional organizations or networks for LGBTQ people in your industry, like Out in Tech for the tech sector or the National LGBT Bar Association for lawyers. These groups offer mentorship, job boards, conferences, and other resources for navigating your career as an out gay person.

Don't hesitate to lean on your personal support system, which includes your queer friends, therapist, partner, or family member. They will not only provide you with an opportunity to vent, but they will also affirm your worth and offer an outside perspective when you're feeling gaslit or beaten down.

Reach out early and often, and let their support fuel your resilience, as you are not alone. An entire community of LGBTQ people is there to make sure that you don’t suffer in silence.

Choose Your Battles

As with homophobia in general, it's important to choose your battles when confronting workplace discrimination. Not every homophobic comment or slight warrants a formal complaint or confrontation. Sometimes the best response is to brush it off and conserve your energy for the bigger issues.

When deciding whether to report or confront homophobia at work, consider factors like:

- The severity and frequency of the discrimination—is it a one-off remark or a persistent pattern of mistreatment?
- The power dynamics at play—is the perpetrator a colleague, a direct supervisor, or a senior leader?
- Potential retaliation or backlash—could speaking up put your job or professional relationships at risk?
- Your own emotional bandwidth—do you have the energy and support to see a complaint process through?
- The likelihood of a positive resolution—based on your company's culture and past handling of discrimination issues, is it likely to be addressed fairly?

Trust your gut and prioritize your own safety and well-being. If something feels too risky or draining to confront head-on, that's okay. Focus on documenting it privately and seeking support elsewhere. Save your voice for the battles that really matter. It is crucial to speak up if you encounter blatant and severe discrimination that affects your performance at the workplace.

In such a case, make sure you report the incident(s) to HR or a trusted manager, along with your documentation. Also, try to file a formal complaint with the EEOC or your state's fair employment agency. Don't do this all alone without legal aid; for that, consult with an employment lawyer about your options for legal recourse. But if you feel things aren't turning in your favor or you fear discrepancies, as a last resort, go public with your story through social or traditional media.

You have the right to do your job free from harassment and discrimination, and your company has a legal and ethical obligation to ensure that. Be mindful that homophobia is never okay in the workplace, and to ensure the preservation of your rights, never trust if you are told that you're overreacting to the situation.

Cultivate a Strong Sense of Self-Worth

When you know in your bones that you are a skilled, competent, and worthy professional regardless of your sexual orientation, other people's biases and bad behavior can't rattle you as easily. You become like a tree with strong roots, bending but not breaking in the face of prejudice. Trusting in your deservingness and self-worth is the ultimate revenge against homophobia.

Some ways to build your professional self-worth as a gay man include keeping a running list of your accomplishments, skills, and positive feedback. Read it often, especially when imposter syndrome or homophobia-induced doubt creep in.

Second, proactively seek out stretch projects, learning opportunities, and ways to add value in your role. It becomes hard to deny your excellence if you grow and contribute professionally.

Third, develop a strong personal brand and network within your field. Speak at conferences, publish articles, and cultivate a stellar LinkedIn presence. Let your expertise and thought leadership speak for itself.

Next, prioritize your own professional development with courses, certifications, mentorship, etc. Invest in your own growth and marketability, regardless of what your current employer offers.

Finally, have a solid backup plan by keeping your resume updated, your network warm, and your skills sharp. Knowing you have options and advocates outside of your current job can give you the confidence to stand up for yourself and set bold boundaries.

Remember, no job or company gets to define your worth as a person or a professional, as that comes from within. You become more immune to the slings and arrows of workplace homophobia if your sense of self-love is stronger. You know the haters are just projecting their own smallness and fear while you're out here shining your brilliant gay light in the world. And if a workplace proves to be hopelessly toxic and homophobic despite your best efforts to change it? Then vote with your feet and find an employer who will celebrate all of you instead of wasting your time and peace of mind in a company that doesn't deserve you.

There are plenty of organizations out there hungry for diverse perspectives and actively cultivating LGBTQ talent. Go where you're valued and set up to succeed. Your dream gay-friendly job is waiting for you. Don't settle for homophobic scraps.

Overcoming Bullying and Harassment

For many gay men, bullying, and harassment are painful realities that start early and persist throughout life. From the schoolyard taunts of childhood to the street harassment and online abuse of adulthood, anti-gay aggressors use physical, verbal, and emotional violence to intimidate, control, and silence us. It's a form of terrorism meant to keep us small, scared, and in line.

The impact of anti-gay bullying can be devastating, resulting in more chances of depression, anxiety, substance abuse, and suicide, according to different studies. In comparison to the straight peers, gays are more likely to skip school, see their grades suffer, and experience health problems into adulthood. Even for grown gay men, the chronic stress of harassment can lead to PTSD, self-loathing, and a diminished quality of life.

Bullying may be a fact of life for many gay men, but that doesn't mean that it has to break us. We can learn to protect ourselves, stand up to aggressors, and even use the pain as fuel for our own empowerment. By developing resilience, self-respect, and community solidarity, we can overcome bullying and come out stronger on the other side.

Some strategies for dealing with anti-gay bullying and harassment are:

Realize That You're Not to Blame

Begin by unlearning all the shame or self-blame for being gay, as no matter what homophobic aggressors may say; you are not provoking or deserving of their abuse simply by existing as a gay person. Their violence is a reflection of their own fear, ignorance, and insecurity, not your worth.

It's easy to internalize the hateful messages we hear from bullies and start to believe them on some level, but the truth is, it's not your fault if someone is being a bigot. We may think if we could just butch up, take up less space, or be less "flamboyant," we could avoid being targeted. Their hate is their own responsibility, not yours.

Remind yourself often that you are entitled to safety, respect, and dignity, period. You do not have to shrink, hide, or apologize for who you are to earn the right to exist in peace. Bullying is never the victim's fault, and anyone who says otherwise is feeding you a toxic lie.

Make Your Safety a Priority

Your physical and emotional priorities come first when dealing with bullying or harassment. In such a case, make sure to walk or run away from the aggressor immediately. Consider the options for escape around you, for example, ducking into a store, restaurant, or other public place. As soon as you reach a safe place, call a friend, family member, or crisis hotline for support. Meanwhile, you can report the incident to authorities only if it's safe to do so. If you are being harassed online, immediately block or report online trolls and abusers. Finally, if you have been physically assaulted, seek medical attention.

It is highly recommended to avoid standing up to bullies or fighting back in the moment, especially if it doesn't feel safe. There will be time for bystander intervention and self-defense training later. Now is the time to strategize immediately to get out of this scary situation and get the support you need to regroup.

Process the emotions, i.e., fear, anger, shame, vulnerability, and grief, after ensuring that you are in a safe space. Let yourself feel them fully, without judgment. Talk to someone you trust about what happened, or write it out in a journal. Be extra gentle and nurturing with yourself as you move through the aftermath, and make sure to discuss the incident with your personal support group or write it in a journal for mental peace.

Establish a Support Network

Your support network is the lifeline in the journey of gayhood, as they have your back in all kinds of untoward circumstances, including bullying, and they also affirm your worth when things get tough.

Some key people to have in your corner:

Other LGBTQ folks who get it. There's nothing like the solidarity and shared understanding of the queer community when you're being harassed for being gay. Lean on your queer friends for empathy, validation, and a reminder that you're not alone.

Straight allies who speak up. Having non-LGBTQ people in your life who are vocal advocates can be incredibly powerful. They can use their privilege to call out homophobia, intervene in bullying situations, and show that being an ally means more than just passive acceptance.

Supportive authority figures. Cultivate relationships with teachers, coaches, bosses, faith leaders, or other authority figures who have your back. Let them know what's been happening and ask for their allyship and protection. Sometimes just knowing an adult is on your side can deter bullies.

LGBTQ organizations and helplines. Get connected with local and national LGBTQ advocacy groups that offer support, resources, and community support for dealing with anti-gay harassment. Save the contact info for crisis hotlines like The Trevor Project in case you need someone to talk to in a moment of distress.

Reach out early and often, and let your people, organizations, and community love you, advocate for you, and support you through it.

Record and Support

It is always wise to write down the date, time, location, and details of each incident, as well as any witnesses who saw or heard what occurred, and also save screenshots, emails, or other evidence if the harassment is digital. But bear in mind that not all incidents are worth it, but your homework will come in handy if things get out of your control and the situation demands reporting.

Having this documentation can be crucial if you decide to report the bullying to the authorities or pursue legal action. The documentation will bolsters your credibility, and reflect a behavioral pattern toward the offender. It also keeps reminding you that the recurrence of incidents is beyond tolerance and you need to take strict action to stop it.

If you feel safe and supported in doing so, consider reporting the bullying to someone in a position of power. That might be a teacher, principal, HR representative, or even the police if the harassment is severe or violent. Share your documentation and any evidence you've gathered, and be clear about the impact it's having on your life.

In some cases, reporting can lead to meaningful consequences for the bully and protection for you and others, and if it is inconsequential, taking a stand for self-protection makes you feel empowered. It sends a message to the aggressor (and to yourself) that you won't be silenced or intimidated into submission.

Practice Self-Defense and Assertiveness

It goes without saying that violence in response to bullying is the last resort in cases where physical defense is the only way out. Look for LGBTQ-specific classes that teach both physical techniques and verbal de-escalation strategies, as taking self-defense training equips you with the skills and confidence to protect yourself in the face of danger.

More often than not, overcoming bullying is about developing assertiveness and learning to stand up for yourself verbally. That means communicating your boundaries clearly, confidently, and consistently—even if your voice shakes.

Some phrases to keep in your back pocket:

- "Do not speak to me that way. It's disrespectful and unacceptable."
- "I don't find your homophobic jokes funny. Please stop making them around me."
- "If you continue to harass me, I will report you to [an authority figure]. This is your only warning."
- "I'm not interested in engaging with you when you're being hateful. I'm walking away now."

Practice saying these kinds of statements in the mirror or with a supportive friend until they start to feel natural. Notice how you carry yourself as you say them—your posture, your eye contact, your tone of voice. Embody the energy of someone who knows their worth and won't be messed with.

It will be easier to stand up to bullies in the moment if you flex your assertiveness muscle. But even if you can't find the words in the heat of harassment, know that your dignity and courage speak volumes. You are stronger than their hate.

Discover Your Joy and Purpose

The most powerful antidote to anti-gay bullying is living your life with authenticity, joy, and purpose. The more you pour your energy into the people, activities, and causes that light you up, the less power bullies have to dim your shine.

Make a commitment to invest in your own happiness and growth, even (especially) in the face of harassment. Double down on your passions and pleasures. Spend time with people who celebrate you. Volunteer for or advocate for an LGBTQ cause you believe in. Create art that tells your story and uplifts your community.

Seek out role models and representations of joyful, thriving gay lives. Read books, watch films, and go to events that depict queer people overcoming adversity and flourishing. Let them be a testament to your own resilience and possibility.

The bullies and bigots of the world want us to be small, scared, broken, and silent. But every time we choose joy over shame and pride over fear, we prove them wrong. We show that their hate is no match for our fierce, fabulous, unbreakable gay spirit, and we deserve to live on.

So keep shining, keep fighting, and keep finding your people and your purpose. Never let anyone dull your glow. You've got this.

Fighting for Legal Rights and Protections

As gay men, our experiences with homophobia, hate, harassment, and discrimination are not just personal; they're political, as the social and legal systems have been dehumanizing and criminalizing us for ages. From sodomy laws to marriage bans to a lack of employment protections, the deck has long been stacked against us.

The most powerful way to combat homophobia is by fighting for our legal rights and protections, as this is the only way to get our equality and humanity recognized, and this is the only way we can chip away at the institutional biases that enable anti-gay discrimination. This is the only way we can create a world where it's not just socially unacceptable to bully and harass LGBTQ people—it's illegal.

Legal change is slow and incremental, and it often feels like we're taking one step forward and two steps back, but every hard-won victory, from the repeal of Don't Ask, Don't Tell to the passage of the Matthew Shepard Hate Crimes Act to the legalization of same-sex marriage, has made life a little bit safer and fairer for LGBTQ people. And we owe those victories to the tireless work of gay activists and allies who refused to accept second-class citizenship.

Many of us want to contribute to getting LGBTQ legal rights. The following are some ways to make your voice heard and push for change:

Stay Informed and Cast Your Vote.

As an effective advocate of your rights, you should keep yourself abreast of issues that impact LGBTQ people. Follow LGBTQ news sources, subscribe to advocacy organizations' email lists, and attend community events and discussions. Keep track of relevant legislation and court cases to learn about the current state of LGBTQ rights in your area and nationally.

Get yourself registered to vote and show up to the polls in every election, not just the big national ones. Research candidates' stances on LGBTQ issues and support those who have a proven record of allyship. Pay attention to judicial races, as the courts play a huge role in deciding our rights.

We can make our voices heard and hold elected officials accountable with the simple act of voting. It's how we choose leaders who will fight for our interests and values. And in a world where many LGBTQ people (especially trans and queer people of color) still face barriers to voting, exercising that right is a radical act.

Lobby Your Representatives

You have the power to influence the people who make effective laws and policies as a constituent, and surprisingly, you don't even need to be a professional lobbyist to lobby your representative. And when enough constituents speak up about an issue, politicians take notice.

Here are some simple ways to lobby your elected officials:

- Email, call, or write letters expressing your views on LGBTQ rights issues by focusing on issues about the bills or policies you support or oppose and how they would impact you personally.

- Attend town halls or other public events where your representatives are present. Ask them direct questions about their stances on LGBTQ equality and push them to take action.
- Schedule an in-person meeting with your representative or their staff. Come prepared with talking points and personal stories to illustrate why LGBTQ rights matter to their constituents.
- Organize a group of constituents to visit your representatives offices together. There's strength in numbers, and seeing a united front of LGBTQ voters can be powerful.

You have the right to be persistent, passionate, and even a little bit annoying in your advocacy as your representatives work for you, and its in their job description to listen to your concerns and issues. The squeaky wheel gets the grease, and the loudest voices often shape the agenda.

Support LGBTQ Advocacy Organizations

People like us can play a vital role by volunteering and providing financial support to organizations like the Human Rights Campaign, Lambda Legal, the National LGBTQ Task Force, and ACLU's LGBTQ Rights Project to do their vital work. Consider making a donation, attending a fundraiser, or signing up to volunteer your time and skills. Many organizations have local chapters or affiliates that you can get involved within your own community.

There is also another way to support LGBTQ advocacy by amplifying these groups' messages and campaigns on social media, in your workplace, and among your friends and family, as there are countless national, state, and local organizations working tirelessly to advance your legal rights. Share their posts, wear their merchandise, and talk about their work at the dinner table. It will get really hard for our opponents to ignore or dismiss us if we make our fight for LGBTQ equality more visible and vocal.

Participate in Direct Action and Protest

It sounds a bit extreme, but sometimes it becomes inevitable to take to the streets and disrupt businesses to get heard. For example, from the Stonewall Riots to the AIDS crisis die-ins to the recent protests against Trump's anti-trans policies, direct action has been a crucial tool in the LGBTQ rights movement. Besides that, you can make your point by participating in marches, rallies, sit-ins, and other forms of peaceful protest as a powerful way to make our demands heard and put pressure on those in power. It is one of the most peaceful but powerful ways to assert your queer existence and your right to equality.

There is always an element of risk involved, especially for LGBTQ people of color and those with other marginalized identities. But it doesn't mean that we give up on our rights as protestors, our rights to buddy up with others for safety, and our right to have a plan in case of arrest or confrontation with police. For an effective outcome, it's important that you look for protest safety and de-escalation trainings in your area or connect with experienced activists who can show you the ropes.

It is absolutely okay; not everyone is able to put their bodies on the line in protest. There are many ways to support direct action without being in the streets—from making signs and providing water to protesters to live-tweeting and documenting events to donating to bail funds for arrested activists. Find a role that feels authentic and sustainable for you.

Narrate Your Story

The fight for LGBTQ legal rights is about making a case for our humanity and dignity in a world that too often denies us both, and by telling our stories and putting a human face to the abstract concept of "gay rights," we can make our fight more effective.

Your voice matters no matter what the context, including coming out to your conservative family members, sharing your experiences with discrimination at a public meeting, or writing an op-ed about how a proposed law would impact your life incredibly. You have to believe that your story has the power to change hearts and minds, to help others feel less alone, and to remind decision-makers of the real lives at stake.

It is also understandable that telling your story can also be scary and emotionally taxing, especially if you've experienced trauma or rejection related to your identity. This is why it's important to prioritize your own safety and well-being above all else by setting boundaries around how and when you share. You don't owe anyone your pain or your private life.

You're part of a long and proud tradition of LGBTQ storytellers and truth-tellers; do speak the truth in service of the greater good. From James Baldwin to Audre Lorde to Harvey Milk, our forebears have used their voices to crack open hearts and change the world. Following their trail, it's our turn to pick up the mantle and keep fighting for a future where every LGBTQ person can live freely, safely, and joyfully.

The road to full legal equality is long and winding, and progress is rarely linear. But we know that every action we take, every story we tell, every vote we cast, and every dollar we donate brings us one step closer. The day will come when we finally have equal protection under the law because of the collective power and resilience of LGBTQ people and our allies, working tirelessly across generations.

So keep showing up, keep speaking out, and keep believing in a better world. Your voice, your vote, and your vibrant queer self are essential to the fight. We can build a future where every gay kid grows up knowing that they're not just tolerated but celebrated under the law. They will have a future where there is nothing else but love and acceptance. The future will be a world where being gay is not just a right but a joy and a gift. That's the world we will win, one brave step at a time.

Chapter 7:

Spirituality and Finding Meaning

Reconciling Faith or Religion and Being Gay

For many gay men, the journey to self-acceptance and happiness is deeply intertwined with questions of faith and spirituality. It is no wonder that so many of us struggle to reconcile our sexual orientation with our spiritual beliefs because the world in which we live is replete with religious beliefs condemning homosexuality. We are stuck in a false dichotomy of having to choose between accepting the truth of our sexual orientation or being true to our faith. It does nothing but leave us feeling torn, conflicted, and even ashamed.

You can absolutely be a happy, thriving gay man and still have a rich spiritual life by being gay. In fact, it is a crucial part of our spiritual journey to embrace our sexuality; it is a way of honoring our authentic selves and connecting with the divine in a deeper, more intimate way.

Of course, getting to that place of integration and peace is often a long and winding road. It requires unlearning the homophobic messages we may have internalized from religious institutions and doing the hard work of redefining our relationship with faith on our own terms. It means grappling with tough theological questions and coming to our own understanding of what God, the universe, or our higher power really thinks about queerness.

You are not alone in a struggle to reconcile your sexuality with your spiritual beliefs, as many LGBTQ people of faith have walked this path before you, and there are countless resources and communities available to support you on your journey. The following tips will help you in this tussle of identity and religious faith:

Recognize That Homophobia Is a Human Invention, Not a Divine One

The homophobic teachings of many religions are a product of human culture and interpretation, not divine will. It is a truth that you need to keep reminding yourself to seek reconciliation between faith and sexuality. People with different agendas have been involved in picking out-of-context passages and mistranslating sacred texts like the Bible and the Quran to suit themselves and their anti-LGBTW agendas.

In reality, the core messages of most religions—love, compassion, justice, and unity—are fundamentally at odds with homophobia and discrimination. Jesus never once mentioned homosexuality, but he did preach radical inclusion and acceptance of society's outcasts. The Quran celebrates diversity as a sign of God's creativity and emphasizes that all humans are equal in the eyes of Allah. The Torah commands us to "love your neighbor as yourself" without exception or caveat.

Homophobia is a choice that religious leaders and communities have made—a choice that says more about their own fear and ignorance than it does about God's will. Religion has been notoriously used as a tool of oppression to enforce the values of flawed human institutions.

Your sexuality is not a sin or a flaw in the eyes of the divine, but it becomes one only due to a human-made system of beliefs. It is a beautiful, natural part of who you are—a gift to be celebrated, not condemned, and there is no need to grapple with religious guilt or shame about being gay.

Do Your Own Spiritual Research and Reflection

One of the best ways to start untangling the knot of religion and sexuality is to do your own deep dive into your faith tradition's teachings on LGBTQ issues with an open mind and heart instead of relying on the pastor's word for it.

As you read, pay attention to the context and historical circumstances in which the supposedly anti-gay passages were written to see the cultural and social reality of time. And how might that have influenced the way the texts were interpreted and applied? Are there other passages that contradict or complicate the anti-gay ones?

Look for LGBTQ-affirming interpretations and commentaries on your faith's teachings. You will find multiple scholars, theologians, and spiritual leaders who project queer positive, liberating, and illuminating insights (Slater & Cornwall, 2022). For reference, you can check out some great resources, including:

"The Queer Bible Commentary," edited by Deryn Guest

"Queer Theology: Beyond Apologetics" by Linn Marie Tonstad

"Radical Love: An Introduction to Queer Theology" by Patrick S. Cheng

"The Gay Disciple: Jesus' Friend Tells It His Own Way" by John Henson

"Queer and Catholic: A Life of Contradiction" by Mark Dowd

You might know some of the resources of sacred texts for reference, but you still have the option to explore alternative options, especially the ones that resonate with your own inner sense of truth and morality. Also, look for which interpretations feel most aligned with your core values and life experiences? Which ones challenge you to expand your understanding of God and spirituality in exciting new ways?

Remember, your faith journey is ultimately between you and the divine, and no one has the right to direct you in terms of how to practice spirituality. Trust your own heart and mind to guide you towards a relationship with the sacred that feels authentic, nourishing, and true to who you are.

Seek Out an LGBTQ-Affirming Spiritual Community

The most challenging part for many LGBTQ people of faith is meeting the spiritual community so that we don't have to hide or downplay our queerness in order to be welcomed in religious spaces. We may experience blatant discrimination, microaggressions, or just a general sense of unease and inauthenticity.

But here's the good news: There are countless churches, synagogues, mosques, and other faith communities out there that are explicitly LGBTQ-affirming. These are spaces where your whole self is not just tolerated but embraced as a beloved child of God, where your sexuality is seen as a divine gift, not a sin or a problem to be fixed.

Finding an LGBTQ-affirming spiritual community can be a total game-changer in terms of reconciling your faith and your sexuality.

Suddenly, you don't have to compartmentalize or censor yourself anymore. You can bring your full, authentic self to your spiritual practice and be surrounded by people who see the divine beauty in your queerness.

Secondly, you can ask other LGBTQ people of faith in your area for recommendations. Chances are, they've done the legwork of finding affirming spaces and would be happy to share their insights.

Thirdly, look for congregations that have gone through a formal process of becoming "Open and Affirming" (in the Christian tradition) or that publicly display Pride flags, rainbow banners, or other LGBTQ-positive symbols.

Finally, attend an LGBTQ-specific spiritual event or retreat, like the Gay Christian Network conference or a Rainbow Sash mass. These can be great places to connect with like minded folks and discover new affirming communities.

You can consider starting your own spiritual group or gathering if you can't find an existing LGBTQ-affirming congregation in your area. It doesn't have to be something big; even a small, informal group in someone's living room can provide powerful nourishment and belonging. You might be surprised by how many other queer folks of faith are out there, longing for a space to call home.

Develop a Personal Connection With the Divine

Reconciling your faith and your sexuality is about cultivating a direct, unmediated relationship with the divine, learning to trust your own experience of God, Spirit, and the universe, and letting that inner knowing guide you towards a spirituality that feels true and right for you. Spirituality for some LGBTQ people means staying connected to the faith tradition of their birth but reinterpreting its teachings in a queer-affirming way. For others, it means exploring new spiritual paths and practices that resonate with their authentic selves. And for some, it may mean creating their own unique blend of beliefs and rituals that honor the many facets of their identity.

To cultivate a relationship with the divine that is based on love, trust, and radical self-acceptance and to let your queerness be a portal to a deeper, more intimate experience of the holy, here are some of the practices that can help deepen your personal connection with the divine:

Meditation and Prayer

Spend time each day in quiet contemplation, opening yourself up to the presence of the sacred. Use affirming mantras or visualizations that celebrate your sexuality as a divine gift.

Nature Communion

Spend time in the natural world, attuned to the beauty and wonder of creation. Let the diversity and resilience of the earth be a reminder of the inherent goodness of your own queer nature.

Creative Expression

Use art, music, writing, or other creative practices as a way to express your spiritual longings and insights. Let your creations be a celebration of your unique queer spirit.

Embodiment Practices

Engage in activities that help you feel fully present and alive in your body, like dance, yoga, or sacred sexuality. Honor your physicality as a temple of the divine.

Service and Social Justice

Look for ways to put your spiritual values into action by serving others and working for justice. Let your faith be a catalyst for creating a more loving, inclusive world for all.

Your queerness is a sacred gift, a unique lens through which you can experience the depth and breadth of the universe's love for you as the same creative power that made the stars and the sea also made you, in all your fabulous gay glory. Your sexuality is not a barrier to divine love but a beautiful expression of it, which is why you are forever held, cherished, and celebrated by a love that transcends all human understanding.

Finding Personal Meaning and Purpose in Life

As gay men, many of us have had to fight hard to discover and assert our identity in a world that often tries to erase or demean us. We've had to unlearn the toxic messages of a homophobic society and come to a place of self-love and acceptance, often against great odds, to find a sense of meaning and purpose in life.

A million-dollar question would be: What does it really mean to have a meaningful, purposeful life as a gay man? And how can we cultivate that sense of direction and fulfillment, even in the face of ongoing challenges and discrimination?

To find meaning and purpose in life, you have to understand your own unique gifts and values, have passions, and have a positive impact on the world around you. The main purpose is to discover what makes you come alive, pursue it with all your heart, and connect it with something larger than yourself, i.e., a cause, a community, a creative project, or a spiritual path, letting it guide and sustain you.

For gay men, finding meaning and purpose can be a particularly powerful and transformative experience, especially in an environment that considers us flawed or sinful with nothing meaningful to offer. When we learn to love and trust ourselves, we discover that we have so much to give—so much beauty, creativity, compassion, and resilience to share with others.

Some ways to start discovering and living into your own unique sense of meaning and purpose as a gay man could be:

Contemplate Your Passions and Values

First of all, get a clear idea of what really matters to you. What are the activities, causes, or ideas that light you up and make you feel most alive? What are the values and principles that guide your choices and actions?

Practice meditation, journal keeping, or even a conversation with trusted friends to reflect on some essential concerns, like: The moments in your life when you felt most fulfilled and energized, and the common threads that ran through those experiences?

These are all clues to your unique purpose and calling. As you reflect, pay attention to the things that keep coming up for you, even if they don't seem directly related to your career or your current life circumstances. Maybe you have a deep love of nature, a passion for social justice, or a knack for making people laugh.

Reflect on the kind of impact you want to have on the world by considering questions like, Do you want to create beauty and joy? Heal suffering and promote compassion? Fight for equality and justice? Inspire others to live more authentically? There are plenty of big and small ways to make a difference.

The key is to identify the passions and values that feel most true and alive for you and start orienting your life around them. Let them be your north star, guiding you towards the people, places, and experiences that will help you live to your fullest potential.

Celebrate Your Queer Strengths and Resilience

Since we have experienced firsthand the pain of exclusion and discrimination, we often have a unique set of strengths and skills that can be a powerful source of meaning and purpose in our lives. We know what it's like to be an outsider, and that can give us a special ability to connect with and advocate for other marginalized groups because we have developed a deep sense of empathy and compassion.

We've also had to cultivate tremendous resilience and adaptability, learning to thrive in a world that isn't always welcoming or safe for us. We can create our own families and communities, find joy and beauty in the face of adversity, and stand up for ourselves and each other with fierce love and courage.

These are all incredible strengths that we can harness to serve a larger purpose. We can use our empathy to build bridges of understanding and compassion across different communities. Use resilience, creativity, and adaptability to persevere through challenges and setbacks and inspire others to do the same.

Strengthen yourself enough to make the shame or marginalization a source of power, resilience, and purpose. By embracing our unique queer strengths and experiences, we can tap into a deep well of meaning and potential that is ours alone.

Discover Ways to Contribute and Create a Positive Impact

Finding ways to give back and make a positive difference in the world through living your purpose can take many different forms, depending on your passions, skills, and resources. You can even volunteer for an LGBTQ youth organization and become a mentor and role model for young people who are struggling with their identity. You can use your artistic talents to create work that celebrates queer joy and resilience and inspires others to live more authentically. It means getting involved in activism and advocacy work, fighting for policies and laws that protect and uplift LGBTQ people.

The key is to find ways to contribute that feel meaningful and aligned with your own unique gifts and passions. It's not about sacrificing your own needs or happiness for some abstract greater good but rather about finding the sweet spot where your own fulfillment and the well-being of others can mutually reinforce each other.

And remember, making a difference doesn't always have to mean big, grand gestures; even every little bit counts, and every act of kindness has a ripple effect reaching out to unpredictable terrains. Sometimes the most powerful acts of service and generosity are the small, everyday ones—the kind word to a stranger, the meal cooked for a sick friend, the $10 donation to a cause you care about.

Foster Awareness and Thankfulness

You can also find meaning and purpose in life by cultivating a deep sense of presence and appreciation for the beauty and wonder of life, even amidst its challenges and imperfections. It happens so often that we miss the charm and possibilities of the present moment only because we get caught up in worries about the future or past regrets.

There are some mindfulness practices that can be made part of your routine, like meditation, journaling, and deep breathing, as they can be powerful tools for learning to stay grounded in the here and now. For the sake of inner peace, quieten your mind and connect to your body and senses to develop a deeper appreciation of simple things in existence, like the taste of a ripe fruit, the sound of laughter, or even the warm touch of sun rays on your face.

Gratitude is another essential practice for finding meaning and purpose, as it helps us acknowledge the existence of things taken for granted and lets us appreciate tiny but good things in our lives. The attitude of appreciation shifts our focus from a sense of deprivation towards the abundance of things that are available to us.

Practicing appreciation could be done by keeping a gratitude journal and by writing down three things you're thankful for each day. Take a moment before each meal to silently give thanks for the food and the hands that prepared it. You can also practice appreciation by making a habit of expressing your appreciation to the people in your life and letting them know how much they mean to you. We can open ourselves up to the possibility of meaning and purpose in every moment by learning to approach life with mindfulness and gratitude. It works wonderfully in changing our perspective on ordinary experiences, as now they look imbued with a sense of sacredness and significance.

Trust the Journey and Stay Open to Growth

Finally, finding meaning and purpose is not a fixed destination; it's rather a process of continual growth, learning, and unfolding as we encounter new experiences and challenges that shape and refine our understanding of ourselves and the world.

One thing we need to realize is that our sense of purpose is always evolving and expanding with the progression of our lives and circumstances. It's quite a useless exercise to put pressure on ourselves to have it all figured out. What felt meaningful and fulfilling at one stage of life may no longer resonate as we enter a new chapter.

Secondly, it is quite pertinent that you stay open and curious and you trust that each step of the journey is unfolding exactly as it's meant to. Instead of getting confused and disoriented, let yourself be surprised by the unplanned twists and turns of life and embrace the mystery and the not-knowing. Stay anchored in your own inner wisdom and intuition, but also be willing to let go of old ideas and identities that no longer serve you. Remember that growth and transformation often involve discomfort and uncertainty, but they also open up new possibilities and adventures that you could never have imagined.

As a gay man, you have already shown incredible courage and resilience in claiming your truth and forging your own path. Trust that the same inner strength and wisdom that have brought you this far will continue to guide you towards your deepest fulfillment and purpose. Stay open to the magic and mystery of the journey, and know that your unique light is needed in this world, now more than ever, as your existence is a testament to the power of love and authenticity, and through this power, you can overcome fears and hate. Keep shining, keep growing, and keep discovering new depths of meaning and purpose in each moment, as the best is yet to come.

Contributing to the Community

An effective way to lead a meaningful life with a deepened sense of connection, empowerment, and self-worth is to support the LGBTQ community, which has supported us in need for an hour. It helps us make a positive difference in the lives of those who need us by simply sharing our time, talents, and resources.

It is the only way we can give back and honor the sacrifices and struggles of the queer elders and activists who came before us. It is their courage and resilience that paved the way for the freedoms and opportunities we enjoy today. We can return or move forward the love and support of the LGBTQ community to create a better, more just, and more compassionate world for the generations of queer people yet to come.

You can give back to the LGBTQ community in a number of ways, depending on your passions, skills, and resources. For instance:

Offer Your Time and Skills

Volunteer your time and energy for LGBTQ organizations and causes by helping out at a local community center, staffing a hotline for queer youth, or organizing a fundraiser for an HIV/AIDS service organization. There are endless opportunities to make a difference through volunteering.

Start by researching LGBTQ nonprofits and community groups in your area and seeing which ones resonate with your interests and values. For that, reach out and attend one of their events to get a sense of their work and culture. If it clicks, ask them about volunteer opportunities. There are many organizations that have specific volunteer programs or positions for which you can apply, while others may be more informal and open-ended.

If you have particular skills or expertise to offer, consider how you can use them in service of the LGBTQ community. For example:

- If you're a writer or graphic designer, you could help create marketing materials or social media content for a queer advocacy group.
- If you're a lawyer or legal professional, you could offer pro bono services to LGBTQ clients facing discrimination or harassment.
- If you're a therapist or counselor, you could volunteer at a mental health clinic that serves LGBTQ patients.
- If you're a teacher or educator, you could lead workshops or trainings on LGBTQ issues for schools, workplaces, or community groups.
- If you're a performer or artist, you could donate your talents to a queer arts organization or fundraising event.

Pick up a volunteer role that feels meaningful and fulfilling to you and that allows you to use your unique gifts and passions in service of others. But it doesn't mean you can't experiment and explore more; don't be afraid to start small or try out different opportunities until you find the right fit. It can create a big difference in the life of an LGBTQ person in need, even by giving a few hours a month.

Serve as a Mentor or Example

Our own experience, wisdom, and example make up a powerful gift for our younger gay fellows. Our guidance and experience can help them navigate their way through the challenges and joys of coming out, building healthy relationships, and finding peace in life.

Mentoring can take many different forms, from formal programs like Big Brothers and Big Sisters to informal relationships with younger folks in your community. You might mentor a queer student who is struggling in school or take a newly out gay man under your wing as he explores the dating scene for the first time. You can become a sounding board for a trans teenager to help them sort out their gender identity. Provide a source of guidance for a young lesbian couple who are grappling with the ups and downs of their first serious relationship.

As a good mentor, listen more than you advise and create a safe, non-judgmental space for your mentee to share their thoughts, feelings, and experiences. It is not recommended to "fix" their problems or impose your own agenda on them—instead, your focus should be on empowering them to find their own solutions and trust their own instincts.

The sharing of your struggles and the lessons learned provides a premise for the mantee to foresee a possibility for a happy, healthy, and successful future for himself. Let them get inspiration from your example of how your triumphs in the face of adversity and discrimination have shaped your life and your worldview.

The act of being visible and proud of who you are delivers a powerful message to young queer people towards self-acceptance and a proud existence. You don't necessarily have to provide one-on-one mentoring, but by simply living your life openly and authentically, you can inspire gay youth to thrive and flourish as their true selves. You never know who might be watching and taking inspiration from your example.

Provide Financial Support or Resources

Financial donations or in-kind contributions to queer-focused organizations and causes are also another way to give back to the LGBTQ community. Your donation doesn't necessarily mean to be a large gift; even small donations go a long way toward helping make a big impact over time. Look for organizations that align with your values and priorities, and that have a track record of making a positive difference in the lives of LGBTQ people (RealSimple, n.d.). You can consider the following:

- LGBTQ youth services and suicide prevention, such as The Trevor Project or the It Gets Better Project.
- HIV/AIDS research, prevention, and care, such as amfAR or the Elizabeth Taylor AIDS Foundation.
- Transgender rights and advocacy, such as the National Center for Transgender Equality or the Transgender Law Center.

- LGBTQ healthcare and mental health services, such as the Callen-Lorde Community Health Center or the Howard Brown Health Center.
- Queer arts and culture, such as the Leslie-Lohman Museum of Art or the Queer Cultural Center.
- International LGBTQ human rights organizations, such as OutRight Action International or the Rainbow Railroad (RealSimple, n.d.).

In addition to monetary donations, you can also give back by donating goods or services to LGBTQ organizations in need. For example, you might donate gently used clothing or toiletries to a homeless shelter that serves LGBTQ youth or offer your professional skills (such as web design or event planning) to a cash-strapped queer nonprofit.

Support LGBTQ-owned businesses and service providers in your community, as by patronizing queer-friendly companies and professionals, you help to create a thriving ecosystem of mutual support and empowerment within the LGBTQ community.

Promote Change

Last but not least, use your voice and influence to advocate for change on a broader scale, which might mean getting involved in grassroots activism and advocacy work, lobbying your elected officials on LGBTQ issues, or using your platform (whether it's social media, a blog, or a public speaking gig) to raise awareness and inspire others to take action.

Some ways to be an effective LGBTQ advocate include:

First, educate yourself on the issues facing the queer community, both locally and globally. It includes staying informed and sharing knowledge with others about current events, legislation, and social movements that impact LGBTQ people.

Secondly, speak out against homophobia, transphobia, and other forms of discrimination whenever you encounter them, including discrimination happening at work, school, or in your own family and social circles.

Thirdly, attending rallies, marches, and other public demonstrations in support of LGBTQ rights and visibility. Show up in person to stand in solidarity with your queer siblings and help to create a critical mass of resistance and resilience.

Fourthly, write letters, make phone calls, and schedule meetings with your elected officials to advocate for pro-LGBTQ policies and legislation. It also includes holding your representatives accountable to the needs and concerns of their queer constituents.

Finally, amplifying the voices and stories of LGBTQ people, especially those who are most marginalized and vulnerable (such as queer people of color, trans women, and LGBTQ refugees and asylum seekers). Use your privilege and platform to lift up those who are often silenced or ignored, and help to create a more inclusive and intersectional movement for queer liberation.

Advocacy is all about building coalitions and collaborating with others who share your vision for a more just and equitable world. You can be most helpful by collaborating with LGBTQ organizations or discovering ways to amplify each other.

It is the recognition that our liberation and well-being are inextricably linked to those of all queer people everywhere. Giving back to your community in the best manner demands using our own gifts, resources, and influence to help create a world where every LGBTQ person can thrive and flourish, free from fear, violence, and discrimination.

We tap into a deep well of meaning, purpose, and connection that nourishes our own souls by giving back. We create a tangible difference by being part of something larger than ourselves—a movement and a community that has been fighting for love, justice, and equality for generations. It provides a greater sense of happiness and satisfaction when we go beyond our needs and desires towards the well-being and empowerment of all those around us.

Nurturing a Spiritual Practice

Cultivating a spiritual practice is an essential part of finding meaning, purpose, and inner peace in life for gay men. Spiritual practice doesn't necessarily means following the traditional rituals of mainstream religion; it rather means building a connection to nature and the universe through religion or personal meditation. The purpose is to develop a sense of something greater than ourselves, as it can provide comfort, guidance, and perspective in the face of life's challenges and uncertainties.

The idea of embracing a spiritual practice may bring up feelings of shame, anger, or rejection and may seem incompatible with being a proud and happy gay man. Unfortunately, it is a result of complicated or even traumatic experiences with religion and spirituality, especially in a conservative society. However, the takeaway from here is that spirituality and religion are not one-size-fits-all, and there are countless ways to cultivate a meaningful and affirming spiritual life as an LGBTQ person. Discover the practices and traditions that resonate with your beliefs, values, and experiences, and the ones that bring you to peace with yourself and the world around you. Begin by developing a customized spiritual practice by following these instructions:

Investigate Various Traditions and Practices

Begin by educating yourself about the different available traditions and approaches. This might involve reading books or articles about various religions and philosophies, attending services or workshops at different places of worship, or talking to friends and mentors about their own spiritual journeys.

Some questions to consider as you explore:

- What are the core beliefs and values of this tradition? How do they align (or not) with my own worldview and life experiences?
- What are the rituals, practices, and observances associated with this tradition? Do they feel meaningful and relevant to me?
- How does this tradition view and treat LGBTQ people? Is there a history of inclusion and affirmation, or a legacy of exclusion and discrimination?
- Are there specific teachers, leaders, or communities within this tradition that I feel drawn to or inspired by? Does their message or approach resonate with me?

Many people find that their spiritual practice is a unique blend of different influences and approaches. You have to keep an open mind and trust your own instincts and experiences as you explore, instead of choosing just one path.

Discover or Build a Supportive Community

You develop a sense of connection and belonging that only comes from being part of a community of like-minded seekers. It provides you with an opportunity to share your spiritual journey with your fellows to learn from, to support, and to be supported by, which can be incredibly nourishing and transformative.

If you're interested in pursuing a particular religious tradition, look for LGBTQ-affirming congregations or communities within that faith. Many denominations have specific groups or ministries for queer members, such as Dignity USA for LGBTQ Catholics or Keshet for LGBTQ Jews. You can even root for different independent churches, synagogues, mosques, and other places of worship that welcome and celebrate LGBTQ people.

If you prefer a more eclectic or secular approach to spirituality, seek out LGBTQ meditation groups, yoga classes, or nature-based gatherings in your area. You can also create your own spiritual community by hosting regular meetups or rituals with friends who share your values and interests.

The key is to find a community where you feel seen, accepted, and supported in your spiritual journey as an LGBTQ person. Don't settle for a group or tradition that asks you to hide or downplay your identity or that treats your queerness as a problem to be fixed, as you deserve to be part of a community that celebrates and affirms all of who you are.

Establish a Personal Routine

It's important to develop a personal practice that you can turn to on a daily or regular basis by setting aside time each day for meditation, prayer, journaling, or other contemplative activities that help you connect with your inner wisdom and sense of purpose.

Some ideas for personal spiritual practices:

- Firstly, start your day with a few minutes of silent meditation or deep breathing, focusing on a particular intention or mantra (such as "I am loved" or "I am enough").
- Secondly, keep a gratitude journal where you write down three things you're thankful for each day, no matter how small or mundane.
- Thirdly, take regular walks in nature, paying attention to the beauty and wonder of the world around you and feeling a sense of connection to something larger than yourself.
- Fourthly, create a sacred space in your home—an altar, a meditation cushion, or a special corner—where you can go to reflect, pray, or simply be still and present.
- Fifthly, read spiritual texts or listen to talks by teachers or leaders who inspire and challenge you, and reflect on how their teachings apply to your own life and experiences.
- Sixthly, engage in creative activities that help you express your spiritual longings and insights, such as writing poetry, making art, or playing music.

The cultivation of a sense of inner peace, resilience, and connection makes you feel authentic and meaningful. There is no right or wrong way of doing it or following someone else's rules—trust your own intuition and let your practice evolve and change over time.

Embrace the Unknown

As LGBTQ people, we may feel a particular urgency around the existential questions, given the discrimination, violence, and marginalization that we face in the world. We may long for a sense of certainty or security in the face of so much adversity and uncertainty. This dilemma puts them in a more vulnerable position of spirituality in terms of existential questions like: What is the meaning of life? What happens after we die? Why do bad things happen to good people? How can we find hope and joy in the face of suffering and injustice?

It is okay not to have all the answers; you have to learn it as part of your spiritual journey. It's about cultivating a sense of trust and surrender in the midst of mystery and paradox, even when things feel scary, confusing, or unfair.

Our job is to show up with love, compassion, and integrity in each moment without giving up on our values or our desire for justice and equality. But you have to recognize that there are forces at work in the universe that are beyond our control or understanding and that demand patience from us regardless of the outcome.

Some ways to cultivate openness and trust in the face of uncertainty are:

- Firstly, practice letting go of attachment to specific outcomes or expectations and focusing instead on the quality of your presence and intention in each moment.
- Secondly, cultivate a sense of curiosity and wonder about the mysteries of life, rather than trying to figure everything out or have all the answers.
- Thirdly, seek out stories, teachings, and examples of people who have found meaning and purpose in the midst of adversity and suffering, and let their resilience and faith inspire you.
- Fourthly, remember that you are not alone in your struggles and doubts, and that countless others have walked this path before you and found their way through.
- Fifthly, trust that even in the darkest and most difficult moments, there is greater wisdom and love at work in the universe and that you are held and supported by something larger than yourself.

Ultimately, cultivating a spiritual practice as an LGBTQ person is about learning to trust your own inner guidance and to find your own way through the wilderness of life.

Seeking an authentic spiritual life is not always easy, and it may involve facing some painful truths and letting go of some cherished beliefs or identities along the way. But it comes with immeasurable rewards like: A sense of peace, joy, resilience, and belonging that can sustain you through even the toughest challenges and darkest nights.

So keep seeking, keep questioning, keep opening your heart to the mystery and beauty of existence, and find consolation in knowing that you are loved, valued, and supported by a power greater than yourself. Trust that your unique journey as an LGBTQ person has a sacred purpose and meaning, even if you can't see it yet.

Chapter 8:

Aging and Growing Older as a Gay Man

Challenges and Joys of Being an Older Gay Man

We often face unique challenges and opportunities as we age and enter our later years. First, we have to grapple with the physical and emotional changes that come with growing older, along with the social stigma and discrimination that can accompany being an LGBTQ elder. Secondly, we also get a new kind of wisdom, resilience, and joy that comes from a lifetime of navigating adversity and embracing our authentic selves.

Older gay men usually feel invisible, devalued, and even shunned by their own peers due to pervasive ageism. This is mainly due to the youth-obsessed culture that often equates beauty and desirability with a narrow range of physical attributes. Older gay men can feel invisible, devalued, and even shunned by their own peers.

This is especially true in gay male spaces and subcultures that prioritize physical appearance and sexual prowess above all else. Older men may feel like they have no place or value and may struggle to find companionship, intimacy, and a sense of belonging, especially in the most popular gay places like bars, clubs, and dating apps. On top of that, many older gay men belong to an age when homosexuality was heavily stigmatized and even criminalized, making them realize that their love was sinful or sick.

Internalized phobia, self-doubt, and a sense of lost time or missed opportunity are natural results among old gay men. It is quite understandable that they may feel vulnerable and weak due to their age, despite the fact that they've had to fight for every scrap of self-acceptance and social support.

On the contrary, being an older gay man can also come with a profound sense of pride, perspective, and purpose because they are the ones who have survived and even thrived in the face of so much adversity and navigated their way to greater acceptance. They have a unique kind of strength, resilience, and wisdom that can be a source of inspiration and guidance for younger generations, being witnesses to incredible progress from the Stonewall Riots to the legalization of same-sex marriage.

Serving as mentors, role models, and chosen family members, older gay men have a reservoir of stories, experiences, and insights to share with those who are just beginning their own journeys of self-discovery and liberation.

Older gay men also have the opportunity to redefine what it means to age and to be an elder in their communities. Rather than buying into the notion that growing older means becoming irrelevant or invisible, they can embrace their age as a badge of honor and a source of authority and influence.

They have been using their perspective to create new spaces and programs that celebrate and support the unique joys and challenges of being an older gay man. They are a reminder to the world that the LGBT community values people of all ages.

The purpose is not to undermine the obstacles that come with aging in a society that still marginalizes and discriminates against LGBTQ people. But to merely embrace the joys and opportunities that are offered to older gay men. But by focusing on the strengths, resilience, and wisdom that come with a lifetime of living authentically, older gay men can find a sense of meaning, purpose, and even happiness in their later years.

Some tips for navigating the challenges and embracing the joys of being an older gay man:

First, seek out community and support specifically for LGBTQ elders, such as social groups, healthcare providers, and housing options that cater to the unique needs and experiences of older gay men.

Second, stay connected to the broader LGBTQ community and look for ways to share your stories, insights, and mentorship with younger generations. Consider volunteering with LGBTQ youth organizations or activism groups.

Third, challenge ageist attitudes and stereotypes whenever you encounter them, both within and outside of the LGBTQ community. Speak out against the idea that older people are asexual, irrelevant, or a burden on society.

Fourth, embrace your age as a source of wisdom, experience, and authority, and use it to advocate for the needs and rights of LGBTQ elders by getting involved in local or national organizations that are working to improve the lives of older LGBTQ people.

Fifth, take care of your physical, mental, and emotional health as you age, and don't be afraid to seek out support or resources when you need them. Prioritize self-care, stress management, and healthy habits that can help you feel your best at any age.

Sixth, find ways to stay engaged, curious, and mentally stimulated as you age, whether through learning new skills, traveling to new places, or pursuing creative hobbies and interests. Embrace the idea that growth and self-discovery are lifelong processes.

Last, cultivate a sense of gratitude and appreciation for the joys and blessings of your life, no matter how small or mundane they may seem, by reflecting on the people, experiences, and accomplishments that have brought you meaning and fulfillment over the years.

Value the old gay man's identity as unique, with challenges and opportunities of its own. You can find a sense of belonging, purpose, and happiness by embracing wisdom and staying connected to your own community.

Maintaining Health, Vitality, and Sexual Well-Being

As gay men age, maintaining optimal health, vitality, and sexual well-being can become increasingly important and challenging. Most gay men suffer from stress, discrimination, and marginalization along with unique risks and obstacles that come with the physical changes of getting older.

Sexual health and function are the main concerns. As the body ages, it undergoes a variety of changes that can impact sexual desire, performance, and satisfaction. Some of the symptoms include a declining level of testosterone, leading to decreased libido, erectile dysfunction, and other sexual issues like an enlarged prostate gland causing urinary problems and discomfort. Besides, other chronic health conditions like diabetes, heart disease, and certain medications can all take a toll on sexual function and enjoyment.

There is always a large probability of getting sexually transmitted infections like AIDS and the specter of HIV. There may have been various ways to prevent or treat HIV in recent decades, but it will always remain a trauma and fear of epidemic years for the older gay men who had to grapple with ongoing stigma in their prime.

The gay male community has long placed a high value on physical attractiveness, sexual prowess, and youthful vigor, which can make the old gay men feel left out, ugly, and rejected in this competitive world. The very realization of being labeled with an "expiration date" or something less relevant or desirable is enough to take a toll on anyone's nerves.

So how can older gay men maintain optimal sexual health, function, and confidence as they age? Here are some tips and strategies to consider:

Prioritize Overall Physical Health and Wellness

Set a goal to take care of your physical well-being by eating a balanced diet, getting regular exercise, doing at least 30 minutes of physical activity, managing stress, and getting enough sleep, as these are all essential for maintaining sexual health and function as we age. At this age, it is wise to focus on whole foods, healthy fats, and plenty of fruits and vegetables.

Talk to Your Healthcare Provider About Sexual Health Concerns

You might feel hesitant due to the stigma attached, but don't be afraid to bring up issues like erectile dysfunction, low libido, or discomfort during sex with your doctor or other healthcare provider. The discussion will be helpful in identifying underlying health conditions or medications that may be contributing to the problem and in recommending treatments or lifestyle changes that can help.

Consider Medications or Other Interventions for Sexual Function

Older men can improve your sexual function and performance through a variety of medications, devices, and other interventions. There are multiple options, like Viagra, Cialis, and testosterone replacement therapy, which can be effective for some men but should always be used under the guidance of a healthcare professional.

Experiment With New Sexual Techniques and Activities

You can experiment with new positions, techniques, or activities that give you the optimum experience. Since you are no longer a younger person, old moves might not be working at this age due to the body's limitations. Focus on sensations and intimacy rather than just performance or orgasm.

Communicate Openly With Partners About Sexual Needs and Desires

Sexual communication becomes more important in old age as our needs and desires change. You can honestly communicate with partners about what feels good, what doesn't, and what you need to feel safe, comfortable, and satisfied in your sexual interactions.

Seek Out Sex-Positive Resources and Support

There are a growing number of resources and communities specifically for older LGBTQ people who want to maintain healthy, fulfilling sex lives as they age. Look for workshops, support groups, or online forums that provide information, advice, and camaraderie for older gay men navigating sexual health and well-being.

Challenge Ageist Stereotypes and Attitudes Around Sex and Desirability

Push back against the idea that older people are asexual, undesirable, or irrelevant in matters of sex and intimacy. You can revert this narrow point of view by embracing your own sexuality and desirability, and by surrounding yourself with people and messages that affirm your right to a healthy, fulfilling sex life as an older gay man.

Of course, maintaining sexual health and well-being is just one aspect of overall health and vitality as we age. It's important to take a holistic approach to wellness that encompasses physical, mental, and emotional health as well during the later years of gayhood.

Some key areas to focus on for overall health and vitality as an older gay man are:

Stay Physically Active and Engaged

To ensure strength, flexibility, balance, and overall health as we age, regular physical activity is essential for maintaining. There are various options that may make you feel happy, like walking, swimming, dancing, or gentle yoga. You can also aim for a mix of cardio, strength training, and stretching to keep your body strong and resilient.

Prioritize Mental and Emotional Well-Being

Prioritize self-care and emotional well-being to avoid the stresses and challenges of being an older gay man, as they can take a toll on mental health. If you are suffering from prolonged stress and anxiety, see a therapist or counselor who specializes in LGBTQ issues. Or you can also join a support group for older gay men or practice stress-management techniques like meditation or journaling (Calmerry, 2023).

Stay Socially Connected and Engaged

In order to cater to loneliness and social isolation, which can be major risk factors for depression, cognitive decline, and other health problems in older adults, you can leave a space in your routine schedule for staying connected to friends, family, and community as you age, whether through social events, volunteer work, or regular check-ins with loved ones. If you don't have many friends and family to mix with, you can consider joining LGBTQ-specific groups or activities that cater to older adults.

Take Care of Your Sexual Health

In addition to the tips mentioned above for maintaining sexual function and satisfaction, it's important to prioritize overall sexual health as an older gay man. This means getting regular check-ups and screenings for sexually transmitted infections, using protection during sexual activity, and communicating openly with partners about sexual health status and needs.

Advocate for Yourself and Your Healthcare Needs

As an older gay man, you may face unique barriers or challenges when it comes to accessing quality, affirming healthcare, and you might have to make an effort to advocate for yourself and your needs with healthcare providers. For that purpose, seek out LGBTQ-friendly or LGBTQ-specific healthcare resources in your community, or even consider working with a geriatric care manager or patient advocate who can help navigate the healthcare system and ensure that your needs are being met.

Embrace a Positive, Proactive Approach to Aging

Rather than buying into negative stereotypes or attitudes about aging, try to embrace a positive, proactive approach to growing older by focusing on the wisdom, resilience, and perspective that come with age, and look for ways to continue learning, growing, and contributing to your community as an older adult. Surround yourself with positive role models and messages about aging, and challenge ageism wherever you encounter it.

Aging is a natural and inevitable part of life, but it doesn't have to be a time of decline or despair. You can maintain a sense of vitality, purpose, and joy well into your later years as a gay man by prioritizing your physical, mental, and sexual health, staying connected to community and support, and embracing a positive approach to growing older.

Confronting Ageism Within the Gay Community

One of the most pervasive and damaging challenges faced by older gay men is the widespread ageism that exists within the LGBTQ community itself. The gay male culture of today often seems to have little room or respect for those who are no longer young, fit, and conventionally attractive, even though the gay rights movement was built on the backs of older activists and trailblazers.

From the imagery and language used in gay media and advertising to the valorization of youth and physical perfection in gay spaces and social circles, the message is clear: To be an older gay man is to be irrelevant, undesirable, and invisible. This toxic culture of ageism robs the entire community of the wisdom, experience, and perspective that our elders have to offer.

So where does this pervasive ageism come from, and what can we do to confront and dismantle it within the gay community? Here is what we can do:

Identify the Origins of Ageism in Gay Male Culture

It's important to first understand where it comes from and how it operates to effectively confront ageism within the gay community. Some of the key factors that contribute to ageism in gay male culture include:

First, there is an emphasis on physical attractiveness and sexual desirability as the primary currency of worth in many gay spaces and interactions. From the idealized images of youth and fitness in gay media to the premium placed on looks and sex appeal in gay dating and hookup culture, the message is often that one's value as a gay man is directly tied to their physical appearance and sexual marketability.

Second, the legacy of the HIV/AIDS epidemic and the trauma of losing an entire generation of gay men in their prime. For many older gay men who lived through the height of the crisis, the specter of illness, death, and grief is still deeply tied to their experience of aging and mortality, which can create a sense of disconnection and resentment among different generations.

Third, there is a lack of positive representation and visibility of older gay men in mainstream media and culture. From film and television to advertising and social media, older LGBTQ people are often either entirely absent or portrayed in stereotypical, negative ways. This lack of diverse, nuanced representation can reinforce the idea that aging is something to be feared or avoided in the gay community.

Fourth, the pressure to conform to heteronormative standards of success and fulfillment as we age. The milestones and markers of a "successful" life—marriage, children, career advancement, and financial stability—have been historically out of reach or fraught with stigma and discrimination for many gay men. This can create a sense of "falling behind" or not measuring up as we enter our later years.

We can start to develop strategies for confronting and dismantling it by understanding the factors that contribute to ageism in the gay community. This involves both challenging the individual attitudes and behaviors that perpetuate ageism and working to change the larger cultural narratives and power structures that uphold it.

Challenge Ageist Attitudes and Behaviors in Yourself and Others

One of the most important things that gay men of all ages can do to confront ageism is to examine and challenge our own biases and behaviors around age and aging. This means:

First of all, we notice when we make assumptions or judgments about someone based on their age, whether that's dismissing an older person's opinions or experiences or assuming that a younger person is naïve or inexperienced. Consciously work to challenge and reframe those assumptions.

Next, be mindful of the language and humor we use around age and aging, and avoid jokes or comments that stereotype or demean older people. Even seemingly harmless phrases like "old queen" or "daddy issues" can reinforce ageist attitudes.

Moreover, we are making an effort to include and value the perspectives and contributions of older gay men in our social circles, workplaces, and community spaces. Actively seek out opportunities to learn from and collaborate with people of different generations.

You can also examine our own internalized ageism and fears around aging and work to cultivate a more positive, accepting relationship with the aging process. This might involve therapy, journaling, or seeking out role models and resources that promote healthy, empowered aging.

Lastly, when we speak up when we witness ageist comments, jokes, or behaviors from others, whether that's in person or online, let him know that ageism is not acceptable or funny and that it harms everyone in the community.

By challenging ageism on an individual level, we can start to shift the larger culture of the gay community towards one of greater inclusion, respect, and solidarity across generations.

Enhance Visibility and Representation of Older Gay Men

In order to confront ageism in the gay community, we must work towards greater visibility and representation of older gay men in media, culture, and public life. This means:

- Supporting and amplifying the voices and stories of older gay men, whether through social media, podcasts, blogs, or other platforms. Seek out and share content that features the perspectives and experiences of LGBTQ elders.

- Advocating for a more diverse and nuanced representation of older gay characters in film, television, and other media. Push back against stereotypical or one-dimensional portrayals and demand stories that show the full complexity and humanity of older gay men's lives.

- Celebrating and honoring the contributions and achievements of older gay men in our community, whether through awards, events, or other forms of recognition. Make it clear that the wisdom, resilience, and leadership of our elders are valued and appreciated.

- Creating and supporting spaces and programs specifically for older gay men to connect, socialize, and share their experiences. This could include everything from social clubs and discussion groups to healthcare and housing resources tailored to the needs of LGBTQ elders.

- Collaborating across generations to create intergenerational dialogue, mentorship, and community building. You can foster opportunities for older and younger men to learn from and support each other.

We can start to shift the narrative around aging and challenge the ageist assumptions and stereotypes that hold us all back by increasing the visibility and representation of older gay men in all aspects of our community and culture.

Advocate for Policies and Structural Changes That Support LGBTQ Elders

Finally, confronting ageism within the gay community requires advocating for policies and structural changes that address the unique needs and challenges faced by LGBTQ elders. This means:

Firstly, fighting for non-discrimination protections and legal recognition for LGBTQ elders in healthcare, housing, employment, and other areas. Ensure that older gay men have equal access to the services and support they need to age with dignity and security.

Secondly, support organizations and initiatives that provide targeted resources and advocacy for LGBTQ elders, such as SAGE (Services and Advocacy for GLBT Elders) or the National Resource Center on LGBT Aging. Donate, volunteer, or spread the word about their important work.

Thirdly, push for greater funding and research into the health and well-being of LGBTQ elders, including issues like social isolation, financial insecurity, and access to affirming healthcare. Advocate for policies and programs that address these disparities and challenges.

Fourthly, working to create more affordable, welcoming housing options for LGBTQ elders, whether through LGBTQ-specific senior living communities or partnerships with mainstream housing providers, ensures that older gay men have safe, supportive places to live and age in the community.

Fifthly, advocating for greater inclusion and representation of LGBTQ elders in mainstream aging services and programs, such as senior centers, meal delivery programs, and caregiver support groups. Push for training and cultural competency around LGBTQ issues among staff and volunteers.

By working towards systemic changes that support and empower LGBTQ elders, we can create a community and a society that values and includes people of all ages and life experiences. This is not just about confronting ageism but about building a world in which every gay man can age with joy, purpose, and dignity.

The confrontation of ageism is an ongoing, multi-faceted process that requires commitment, compassion, and courage from all of us. It means examining our own biases and behaviors, challenging the cultural narratives that devalue and dismiss older people, and advocating for the rights and well-being of LGBTQ elders in all aspects of life. It means building a community that truly celebrates and includes people of all ages and that recognizes the invaluable contributions and perspectives of our elders. We can create a gay culture that is more just, more inclusive, and more empowering for everyone by working together across generations.

Finding Love, Connection, and Support Networks

As gay men age, one of the most important factors in maintaining health, happiness, and quality of life is having strong social connections and support networks. You can weigh your options among a romantic partner, close friendships, family of choice, or community groups. Having people in our lives who love, understand, and support us is essential for both practical and emotional well-being.

However, for many older gay men, finding and sustaining these connections can be a challenge. Due to a lifetime of stigma, discrimination, and marginalization, many LGBTQ elders may have lost or become estranged from family members, struggled to form lasting romantic partnerships, or felt disconnected from the broader gay community. Additionally, as we age, our social circles may naturally shrink as friends pass away, move away, or become less mobile.

Despite these challenges, it's never too late to build new connections, find love, and cultivate a supportive network as an older gay man. Some strategies and considerations for creating the social and emotional support you need to thrive include:

Look for LGBTQ-Specific Groups and Resources

Seek out groups, organizations, and resources specifically geared towards LGBTQ elders to find connection and support as an older gay man. These can provide a sense of community, shared understanding, and tailored support that may be harder to find in mainstream spaces. Some examples include:

First, there are LGBTQ senior centers or community groups, which offer social activities, classes, meals, and other programs for older adults. Many cities have dedicated LGBTQ senior centers or offer LGBTQ-specific programming within larger senior centers.

Second, LGBTQ aging organizations, such as SAGE or the LGBT Aging Project, provide a range of services and advocacy for older LGBTQ adults, including support groups, legal and financial assistance, and healthcare resources.

Third, LGBTQ-affirming religious or spiritual communities can provide a sense of belonging, purpose, and spiritual support for older gay men. Many denominations now have LGBTQ-specific congregations or outreach programs.

Fourth, LGBTQ social and recreational groups, such as sports teams, book clubs, travel groups, or hobby-based organizations, can be a great way to meet new friends, stay active and engaged, and explore shared interests.

Fifth, online forums, social media groups, and dating sites geared towards older LGBTQ adults can provide a way to connect with others from the comfort of home, especially for those with mobility or transportation challenges.

Older gay men can find a sense of belonging, validation, and support that may be harder to come by in mainstream settings by seeking out these LGBTQ-specific resources and communities. It's a way to connect with others who share similar life experiences, challenges, and joys, and to build a network of people who understand and appreciate you for who you are.

Cultivate Intergenerational Connections

Another important strategy for building social connections as an older gay man is to cultivate intergenerational relationships and communities. Rather than only seeking out peers of the same age, look for opportunities to connect with LGBTQ people of all generations—whether that's through mentorship, friendship, activism, or shared interests.

Some benefits of intergenerational connections for older gay men include:

First, learning from the perspectives and experiences of younger LGBTQ people and staying engaged with new ideas, trends, and social movements. This can help keep you feeling vibrant, relevant, and connected to the broader community.

Second, sharing your own wisdom, stories, and life lessons with younger generations and feeling a sense of purpose and value in passing on your knowledge and experience. Many younger LGBTQ people are eager to learn from and be mentored by their elders.

Third, building a more diverse and resilient support network with people of different ages and life stages who can offer a range of practical and emotional support. Younger friends may be able to help with physical tasks or technology, while older friends may offer sage advice and perspective.

Fourth, by challenging ageist stereotypes and assumptions, both within yourself and in the larger community, and by forming authentic, reciprocal relationships with people of all ages, you can help break down the barriers and prejudices that often divide us.

Some ways to cultivate intergenerational connections as an older gay man might include:

First, volunteer with LGBTQ youth organizations or programs, such as GLSEN, The Trevor Project, or PFLAG. Offer to be a mentor, tutor, or simply a listening ear for younger people navigating their own identity and challenges.

Second, attend intergenerational LGBTQ events and programs, such as Pride celebrations, community forums, or activist groups. You can also look for opportunities to engage with and learn from people of all ages and backgrounds.

Third, join social or hobby groups that attract a mix of ages, such as a gay men's chorus, a queer hiking club, or an LGBTQ film society. Don't assume that certain activities are only for young people—you might be surprised by the diversity of participants!

Fourth, reach out to younger LGBTQ people in your personal networks, whether that's family members, coworkers, neighbors, or friends of friends. Offer to grab coffee, share a meal, or simply have a conversation about your experiences and perspectives.

Older gay men can build a richer, more vibrant, and more sustainable support network that includes people of all ages and life stages by actively seeking out and nurturing intergenerational connections. It's a way to stay engaged, challenged, and inspired, and to contribute your own unique gifts to the larger LGBTQ community.

Take Initiative in Dating and Building Romantic Relationships

A top priority and a key component of overall happiness and well-being is finding love and intimacy. It's important to be proactive and intentional in your approach, whether you're seeking a long-term partnership, a casual companion, or simply the opportunity to date and explore new connections.

Some tips for dating and forming romantic connections as an older gay man:

First, get clear on what you're looking for in a partner or relationship, and communicate that clearly in your dating profiles, conversations, and interactions. Don't be afraid to state your needs, desires, and deal-breakers upfront.

Second, be open to meeting people through a variety of channels, including online dating sites, social events, hobby groups, volunteer programs, and mutual friends. Cast a wide net and be willing to step outside your usual comfort zone.

Third, take the initiative to reach out, make plans, and follow up with potential dates or partners. Don't wait around for someone else to make the first move; be bold and proactive in your pursuit of connection.

Fourth, be authentic, honest, and vulnerable in your interactions with potential partners. Share your true self, your hopes and fears, your passions and quirks. Deep connection comes from genuine openness and transparency.

Fifth, take things at a pace that feels comfortable and safe for you, and don't feel pressured to rush into physical intimacy or commitment if you're not ready. It's okay to take your time getting to know someone and building trust gradually.

Sixth, communicate openly and directly about your needs, boundaries, and expectations in dating and relationships. Instead of assuming that your partner can read your mind, be explicit about what you want and need to feel fulfilled and secure.

Lastly, be willing to work through challenges and conflicts that arise in your relationships, whether that's through honest conversation, compromise, or seeking outside support like couples therapy. All relationships require effort and growth to thrive.

Remember, dating and forming romantic connections as an older gay man can come with unique joys and challenges. With maturity, experience, and a sense of responsibility, you may have a clearer sense of what you want. Be patient, compassionate, and persistent in your search for love, and trust that the right person and relationship will come along in due time.

Foster a Healthy Relationship With Yourself

Finally, connection and support as an older gay man is nurturing a strong, loving relationship with yourself is a crucial factor in finding love. You must first develop a foundation of self-awareness, self-acceptance, and self-care before you can build healthy, fulfilling relationships with others. Some ways to strengthen your relationship with yourself as you age are:

First, practice regular self-reflection and introspection, whether through journaling, therapy, meditation, or simply quiet time alone. Get curious about your own thoughts, feelings, needs, and desires without judgment or shame.

Second, cultivate self-compassion and kindness towards yourself, especially in moments of struggle or setback. Treat yourself with the same tenderness and understanding you would offer a beloved friend.

Third, set boundaries and advocate for your own needs and well-being, even when it's difficult or uncomfortable. Learn to say no to people and situations that drain or deplete you and yes to those that nourish and inspire you.

Fourth, develop a strong sense of self-identity and purpose beyond your relationships or roles with others by exploring your passions, values and goals, and pursuing activities and experiences that bring you joy and fulfillment.

Fifth, practice good self-care, including regular exercise, healthy eating, sufficient sleep, stress management, and preventive healthcare. Treat your body and mind with respect and compassion, and prioritize your own well-being.

Lastly, seek out therapy, coaching, or other forms of professional support when needed to work through past traumas, present challenges, or future aspirations. Don't be afraid to ask for help and guidance in your journey of self-discovery and growth.

You create a solid foundation from which to build healthy, reciprocal relationships with others by nurturing a strong, loving relationship with yourself. You become less dependent on external validation or approval and more capable of setting boundaries, communicating your needs, and attracting partners who truly see and appreciate you for who you are. No matter what your relationship status may be, you develop the resilience, self-trust, and inner peace to weather the ups and downs of dating and relationships and to find joy and fulfillment within yourself. The most important love story of your life is the one you have with yourself. By tending to that relationship with care, curiosity, and compassion, you open the door to deeper connection and support in all areas of your life.

It is always possible to find love, connection, and support, even for an older gay man. You can nurture a strong relationship with yourself by seeking out LGBTQ-specific resources and communities, cultivating intergenerational connections, and being proactive in dating and romance. There is always a possibility to build a rich, vibrant network of social and emotional support that will sustain you through the joys and challenges of aging. There is no age limit when it comes to making new friends, falling in love, or discovering new parts of yourself. Embrace the journey with openness, courage, and self-compassion, and trust that the connections and support you need will find their way to you in perfect timing.

Conclusion

As we come to the end of this exploration of how to be a happy and gay man, I hope that you're feeling a sense of hope, empowerment, and possibility. The book has talked in detail about the many joys and challenges of living life as a gay man in today's world. It encompasses the journey of a gay man, from the process of coming out and accepting yourself to building supportive relationships and communities. It also explores the complex life of a gay man, from navigating the complexities of sex, dating, and love to finding meaning and purpose as you age and grow.

I hope that the insights and strategies shared in this book have given you a greater sense of clarity, confidence, and connection on your own path, since the journey of being a gay man is never a simple or straightforward one; rather, it is wrought with ups and downs of its own. Keeping in view the nuanced life of a gay man, the goal of writing this book was not to prescribe a comprehensive and holistic formula for gay happiness but rather to offer a framework and a set of tools that you can adapt and apply to your own unique circumstances and desires.

The message of this book is quite simple and builds you to view yourself as somebody who is perfect as it is, along with his life choices. It helps you understand that your gayness is not a flaw or a burden but a beautiful and essential part of who you are. Just like any other human on the face of the world, you deserve to live a life of authenticity, joy, love, and fulfillment. And you deserve it, not despite being gay, but because of it.

It is true that embodying this truth is often easier said than done, as we live in a world that still often tells us that being gay is something to be ashamed of. It is something that we need to hide or overcome. Although we may have to struggle with internalized homophobia, rejection from family and friends, discrimination in the workplace, or a lack of representation and visibility in mainstream culture, we come off as resilient and powerful advocates of equality and justice. There is pressure to conform to narrow stereotypes of what a "good" or "successful" gay man should look like or feel like, but there is nothing to be worried about if we're constantly falling short of those impossible standards.

The book advocates that the passage to gay happiness and resilience lies not in trying to fit into someone else's mold. It rather lies in learning to love and accept ourselves fully, just as we are. The real deal is about having the courage to live our truth, even when it's hard or scary. Against all the odds and the hatred, we can lead a fulfilling life by surrounding ourselves with people and communities who celebrate and affirm us and letting go of those who don't. The book teaches you how to explore and express our sexuality in ways that feel authentic and empowering to you, without shame or apology. It helps us find meaning and purpose in our lives that goes beyond just our sexual orientation but still honors and includes it as an essential part of life.

In order to lead a happy and purposeful life, the secret lies in embracing the journey of self-discovery and growth, with all its twists, turns, and challenges along the way. It's about having compassion for ourselves when we stumble or struggle and celebrating ourselves when we triumph and thrive. You have to accept the fact that coming out and living authentically is a lifelong process, not a one-time event and that each stage of that process brings its own unique opportunities for joy, connection, and transformation, including challenges.

When you reflect on your own journey as a gay man, I encourage you to take a moment to appreciate how far you've already come. Think back to the early days of first realizing or acknowledging your attraction to other men. Look back at your initial journey, imbued with the fear, the confusion, and the loneliness that you may have felt. At that time, you must have been wondering if you would ever be able to live a full and happy life as a gay person. But if you compare your initial journey with your present state, you must wonder and appreciate—how much you've learned and grown, how many people you've touched and been touched by, and how much more comfortable and confident you feel in your own skin. It was no one but you, as a person, who deserve credit for the courage and resilience that you acquired on the way to this point and for all the ways you've already defied the odds and created a life worth living as a gay man.

The journey doesn't end here. I invite you to get excited about the one still ahead of you, as there is still a lot to experience, new relationships to discover and hold onto, and hidden parts of yourself to discover and embrace. There is always more to explore and uncover on this path, even if you are old in this journey, how "out" you are, or how much you think you have already found out about being gay. In this diverse and complex road towards being gay, each stage of life as a gay man brings its own set of joys, challenges, and opportunities for growth. It uncovers steps from coming out to falling in love to building a career to aging with grace. Get ready to approach each new chapter with curiosity, openness, and a willingness to be surprised and transformed.

Keep reminding yourself that you are part of a rich and vibrant community with a long and proud history of resistance, resilience, and joy—a history that is replete with the ups and downs of your own gay journey. It is history that is replete with examples of gay activists, including the early gay rights pioneers like Marsha P. Johnson and Harvey Milk, and the brave activists and advocates fighting for our rights and dignity today. It also includes countless ordinary LGBTQ people living their lives with authenticity and courage every day. You are not alone in this struggle for self-assertion and equality; you are one strong part of this beautiful and diverse tapestry, woven together by a common thread of love, pride, and perseverance. You have multiple role models to draw strength and inspiration from the stories and examples of those who have come before you, and you know that your own story is an essential part of that ongoing legacy.

It might feel like you are alone, but you are not alone in this, as there are countless other gay men out there who share your fears, your hopes, your triumphs, and your struggles. There is nothing that can stop you or discourage you from reaching out for support, guidance, and community support when you need it. There are multiple options, including LGBTQ organizations, online forums, therapy or counseling, or simply heart-to-heart conversations with friends and loved ones. Your ultimate power lies in building a strong and diverse network of social and emotional support, as it is one of the most important things you can do to thrive as a gay man at any age or stage of life.

I hope that this book has reminded you of your own inherent worth, beauty, and power as a gay man. No matter what messages you may have internalized from family, society, or religion about being gay, know that you are exactly as you are meant to be. The book infuses self-worth, enabling you to take your sexuality as a gift, not a curse—a unique and precious part of your identity that allows you to love, desire, and connect with others in ways that are passionate, intimate, and fulfilling.

As a gay man myself, I am aware of firsthand the joys and struggles of walking this path. I share the experience of questioning your identity, self-worth, loneliness, and finally, the feeling of wondering if you'll ever find love or acceptance, grappling with shame and self-doubt, and facing rejection and discrimination simply for being who you are. But the experience isn't only about being deserted and hopeless; it is ripe with incredible resilience, courage, and heart of our community, and the ways that being gay has made me a more empathetic, authentic, and purposeful human being. I wouldn't trade my gay identity for anything because it has given me a perspective and a passion for life that I cherish deeply.

My hope for you, dear reader, is that you, too, can come to embrace and celebrate your gayness as one of the best things about you with its challenges. I hope that you will network with people and experiences that affirm your identity and your right to respect and be respected without hiding your true self. I hope that you will have the courage to live your truth despite the hurdles and to stand for yourself fully and authentically in every area of your life. I hope that you will dig your own unique way to create an impact and leave a legacy as a proud gay man in whatever way feels purposeful and fulfilling to you.

I hope that you will prioritize your own joy and betterment and make choices that acknowledge your gay self in body, mind, and spirit. You'll take the time to develop a loving bond with yourself, a bond that is full of self-compassion, self-care, and self-discovery. This book prepares you to pursue your passions and curiosities with enthusiasm and let yourself experience all the pleasure, joy, and adventure that life has to offer. You'll build a community of chosen family who see you, love you, and have your back, no matter what. I hope that you make a resolution to never settle for anything less than a life that lights you up from the inside out simply because you're a gay man living it.

At the end of the day, this journey of being a happy gay man is all about learning to love, honor, and celebrate yourself fully. The book prepares you to move through the world with authenticity, integrity, and joy. It gives you the courage to be who you are, to desire what you want, and to accomplish it with all your heart and soul. It enables you to recognize that your sexual orientation is not a sin or sickness but an authentic, pure, and essential part of what makes you uniquely you—and that by accepting it fully, you open yourself up to a world of possibility, connection, and fulfillment.

This journey of gay self-love and empowerment is not always an easy one, as there will be times when you indulge in self-doubt, when you feel like surrendering, and when the weight of homophobia and heterosexism feels like too much to endure. There will be times when you're tempted to hide or shrink yourself to fit in, to settle for crumbs instead of holding out for the whole damn cake. Eventually, when the loneliness, the rejection, the fear, and the pain feel overwhelming, you wonder if it's all worth it.

I hope you'll remember the words of the pioneering gay writer and activist E.M. Forster, who said, "I have only one life, and I will not be ashamed of it." I hope you'll remember that by leading your life with true pride as a gay man, you are not only healing and empowering yourself—you are also paving the way for future generations of LGBTQ people to live more freely and joyfully. I hope you'll remember that every act of self-love and self-acceptance as a gay person is a radical and revolutionary act, one that challenges the status quo and makes the world a little bit brighter and more beautiful for all of us.

So keep going, my friend. Keep loving yourself fiercely and unapologetically. Keep surrounding yourself with people and experiences that celebrate and affirm your gay self. Keep pushing through the fear and the discomfort to live your truth, in ways big and small. Keep seeking out joy, pleasure, and meaning in your life and savoring them with all your heart and soul. Keep believing that you are worth fighting for and that a life of authentic gay happiness is possible for you.

You are part of a vast and nuanced community of millions of LGBTQ people around the world, each walking our own unique path to joy and fulfillment. Know that you are loved, valued, and acknowledged just as you are by a force much greater than yourself. And know that every step you take on this journey of being a happy gay man is a reward, not just to yourself but to the world, because the world needs more people like you, glowing their light and living their truth with bravery, compassion, and happiness.

So here's to you, my gay brother—to the beautiful, brave, and boundless being that you are. May you always remember how wonderfully and uniquely created you are as a gay man. May you find the strength, the support, and the self-love to navigate the ups and downs of this wild and precious life with grace, resilience, and pride. May you have the courage to let your true gay self shine in all your fabulous glory. And may you always know, deep in your bones, that you are enough—exactly as you are—and that a happy, fulfilling, joyful gay life is yours for the taking.

With all my gay love and solidarity,

Jeffrey Yerkey

LGBTQ Resource List

Many incredible organizations, programs, and media outlets are working to support LGBTQ+ communities, advance equality, and provide helpful resources.

Here is just a sampling of some great ones to check out and get involved with:

LGBTQ+ Advocacy Groups

- The Trevor Project: Crisis intervention/suicide prevention for LGBTQ+ youth
- GLAAD: Advocates for fair media representation of LGBTQ+ community
- Lambda Legal: Pursues litigation protecting LGBTQ civil rights
- Human Rights Campaign: Advocates politically for LGBTQ+ equality
- PFLAG: Support for parents/families of LGBTQ+ loved ones
- Athlete Ally: Eliminates homophobia/transphobia in sports

National Hotlines

- GLBT National Hotline: Peer support, counseling, and local resources

- The Trevor Project Lifeline: Crisis intervention/suicide prevention for LGBTQ youth
- Trans Lifeline: By and for transgender people struggling with suicidal thoughts

Online Forums

- Reddit LGBTQ+ Community: Discuss LGBTQ life with 760K+ members
- Empty Closets: Online coming out support and general discussion

LGBTQ+ Media

- Autostraddle: News/culture site for queer women & nonbinary folks
- GLAAD Media Institute: Resources for fair coverage of the LGBTQ community
- Pride.com: Podcasts, blogs, and news on LGBTQ life
- Advocate: Leading LGBTQ news source since 1967

The 10 largest LGBTQ Community Centers in the United States

1. Los Angeles LGBT Center (Los Angeles, CA)
2. New York LGBT Center (New York, NY)
3. Chicago LGBT Center (Chicago, IL)
4. San Francisco LGBT Center (San Francisco, CA)
5. LGBT Center of Central PA (Harrisburg, PA)

6. Milwaukee LGBT Community Center (Milwaukee, WI)
7. Northalsted Business Alliance (Chicago, IL)
8. Sacramento LGBT Center (Sacramento, CA)
9. Rainbow Community Center of Contra Costa County (Concord, CA)
10. Pride Center of Vermont (Burlington, VT)

Some Essential Services These Major Community Centers Provide

- Health services like HIV/STI testing, counseling, and support groups
- Youth and senior programs
- Cultural and social events
- Legal services and advocacy
- Job skills training and career support
- Support groups and hotlines
- Library and archival records
- Shelter and transitional housing
- Arts and cultural events
- Anti-violence and anti-bullying initiatives
- Community meeting spaces and galleries

The 20 of the Largest LGBTQ Community Centers in the World Outside of the United States

1. Pride Centre of Edmonton (Edmonton, Canada)
2. LGBT Foundation (Manchester, UK)
3. Toronto LGBT Community Centre (Toronto, Canada)
4. Café Fuglen (Oslo, Norway)
5. Federation of LGBT People in Norway (Oslo, Norway)
6. Gay and Lesbian Community Center (Mexico City, Mexico)
7. Gay Men's Health Centre (Sydney, Australia)
8. Lesbian and Gay Community Services Center (New York City, USA - a non-profit based in NYC but serves internationally)
9. London Friend (London, UK)
10. Metropolitan Community Church of Toronto (Toronto, Canada)
11. Pink Dot (Singapore)
12. Rainbow Health Victoria (Melbourne, Australia)
13. RFSL National Organization for LGBT Rights (Stockholm, Sweden)
14. Switchboard LGBT+ Helpline (London, UK)
15. Taiwan LGBT Center (Taipei, Taiwan)
16. The 519 (Toronto, Canada)

17. Birmingham LGBT Centre (Birmingham, UK)
18. Center Link: The Community of LGBT Centers (Fort Lauderdale, USA - serves over 200 LGBTQ community centers internationally)
19. Gay & Lesbian Switchboard of Miami (Miami, USA - serves Southern Florida and Latin America)
20. Jerusalem Open House for Pride & Tolerance (Jerusalem, Israel)

These organizations provide many vital services to local LGBTQ populations, including healthcare, counseling, social events, advocacy, education, training, hotlines, and safe community spaces. They empower and support LGBTQ people globally.

References

A quote by Anaïs Nin. (n.d.). Goodreads. https://www.goodreads.com/quotes/348178-shame-is-the-lie-someone-told-you-about-yourself

Corinna, H. (2010, November 11). *Legit or Unfit? Finding Safe, Sound Sex Educators & Support Online.* Scarleteen. https://www.scarleteen.com/read/culture/legit-or-unfit-finding-safe-sound-sex-educators-support-online

I Am Amazing. (2016, October). Self Love Beauty. https://selflovebeauty.com/2016/10/i-am-amazing/

Kerlin, D. (2023, January 10). *The 13 best gay dating apps and sites of 2023 to join when looking for LGBT relationships.* The Telegraph. https://www.telegraph.co.uk/family/relationships/best-gay-dating-apps-sites-lgbtq/

Lambdalegal. (n.d.). *Who We Are.* Protected & Served? Retrieved July 2, 2024, from https://www.protectedandserved.org/who-we-are#:~:text=Lambda%20Legal%20is%20the%20oldest

Liptak, A. (2020, June 15). *Civil Rights Law Protects Gay and Transgender Workers, Supreme Court Rules.* The New York Times. https://www.nytimes.com/2020/06/15/us/gay-transgender-workers-supreme-court.html

Mental and Emotional Issues That Affect Men's Sexual Health. (2023, May 17). Calmerry.com.

https://calmerry.com/blog/relationships/8-mental-and-emotional-issues-that-affect-mens-sex-lives/

Mitchell, J. W., Lee, J.-Y., Woodyatt, C., Bauermeister, J., Sullivan, P., & Stephenson, R. (2016). Decisions About Testing for HIV While in a Relationship: Perspectives From an Urban, Convenience Sample of HIV-Negative Male Couples Who Have a Sexual Agreement. *Archives of Sexual Behavior, 46*(4), 1069–1077. https://doi.org/10.1007/s10508-016-0807-2

National Association for Law Placement | LGBTQ Organizations. (n.d.). NALP. https://www.nalp.org/lgbtq_organizations

Newcomb, M. E., Moran, K., Feinstein, B. A., Forscher, E., & Mustanski, B. (2018). Pre-Exposure Prophylaxis (PrEP) Use and Condomless Anal Sex. *JAIDS Journal of Acquired Immune Deficiency Syndromes, 77*(4), 358–364. https://doi.org/10.1097/qai.0000000000001604

Povey, J. R. (2023, April 28). *This. The ethical pornography movement is something anyone who is interested in consuming porn.* Medium. https://jenniferrpovey.medium.com/this-the-ethical-pornography-movement-is-something-anyone-who-is-interested-in-consuming-porn-73c6e9be6d6d

Schifter, M. (2021, May 17). *3 ways to protect LGBTI rights across the world.* World Economic Forum. https://www.weforum.org/agenda/2021/05/3-ways-to-protect-lgbti-rights-across-the-world/

Slater , J., & Cornwall, S. (2022). *Queer Theology.* St Andrews Encyclopaedia of Theology. https://www.saet.ac.uk/Christianity/QueerTheology

The Joy of Gay Sex: Fully Revised and Expanded Third Edition: Silverstein, Charles, Picano, Felice: 9780060012731. (2024). Amazon. https://www.amazon.com/Joy-Gay-Sex-Revised-Expanded/dp/0060012730

The Velvet Rage: Overcoming the Pain of Growing Up Gay. (n.d.). Goodreads. Retrieved July 17, 2024, from https://www.goodreads.com/book/show/49418.The_Velvet_Rage

Thomas, M. (2023, April 1). *Even if you're "on the apps," it feels pretty hard to meet people these days.* The Guardian. https://www.theguardian.com/commentisfree/2023/apr/02/even-if-youre-on-the-apps-it-feels-pretty-hard-to-meet-people-these-days

20 LGBTQ+ Organizations You Can Support Right Now. (n.d.). Real Simple. https://www.realsimple.com/work-life/lgbtq-organizations-to-donate

Victoryfund.org. (2019, July 22). *LGBTQ Victory Fund.* LGBTQ Victory Fund. https://victoryfund.org/